SANJEEV KAPOOR

LOW-SALT COOKBOOK

In association with Alyona Kapoor

Popular Prakashan
www.popularprakashan.com

Published by
POPULAR PRAKASHAN PVT. LTD.
301, Mahalaxmi Chambers
22, Bhulabhai Desai Road
Mumbai 400 026
for KHANA KHAZANA PUBLICATIONS PVT. LTD.

First Published 2013

(4404)
ISBN: 978-81-7991-656-8

Design: Anjali Sawant
Photography: Bharat Bhirangi & Sanjeev Nadkarni

Printed in India
by G.H. Prints Pvt. Ltd.
A-256, Okhla Industrial Area
Phase 1, New Delhi - 20

Contents

Author's Note

Daily diet plays a very important role in not only keeping us healthy and energetic but also helps in maintaining well-being.

It is the basic need of man to eat for sustenance. Food keeps us well and food also can help us feel better in case the body sends a red alert. One of these red alerts is high blood pressure or hypertension. If you have high blood pressure, the first aim is to try to lower the elevated blood pressure. You need to select your foods properly, and go in for a diet that is varied and adequate in all nutrients, including vitamins and minerals. Also suggested is intake of food that has low sodium levels. This is where daily eating habits play an important role. When one cooks meals using less salt initially it requires some adjustment of the palate, but with time, even low-salt food becomes acceptable. Reducing sodium intake lowers blood pressure in people with hypertension and in people with borderline high blood pressure. Reducing sodium intake also decreases the likelihood that hypertension will return in people who stop taking anti-hypertensive drugs.

This book has been designed to give you access to a variety of foods that allow you to plan your daily intake of sodium. No food is taboo, but if you study the sodium content of your choice of recipe per portion, aim to plan your menu in such a way that your total intake of sodium per day hovers around 1500 mg maximum.

To treat hypertension one would have to follow the physician's recommendations and if necessary reduce or avoid salt in one's diet. To prevent hypertension, however, start by reducing salt in one dish at a time, one meal at a time. This book has some amazing recipes that help you bring out the full flavour of the dish in the best way possible even though the salt used is minimal. Cooking techniques should focus on low oil consumption too. We also suggest you avoid use of frozen prepared foods, or tinned foods or convenience foods. Be cautious and read labels of packaged foods for information on sodium and salt content. Other suggestions are to not use added salt at the table. Use herbs and spices to flavour food. Lemon juice or tamarind juice added to food can also help to increase taste without adding much salt. Make use of black pepper and ginger to enhance taste. Most importantly, do consult your physician before making any changes in your diet.

It is popularly believed that high blood-pressure strikes after 40 which is a misconception. The best way to avoid it is by leading a stress-free life as far as possible, eating a healthy diet, exercising regularly and having regular health check-ups. Here, in the following pages, is a selection of recipes from all courses that are cooked using less salt. All recipes serve four people and complement other dishes in a meal.

Happy Cooking!

Sanjeev Kapoor

Hare Moong Ka Shorba

Sodium Content Per Serving: 354 mg

INGREDIENTS

¾ cup sprouted green gram

½ tablespoon oil

½ teaspoon cumin seeds

1 spring onion, chopped

1 inch ginger, chopped

3 green chillies, chopped

1½ tablespoons lemon juice

½ cup cooked semolina vermicelli

½ level teaspoon salt

6-8 black peppercorns, freshly crushed

METHOD

- Pressure-cook the sprouted green gram along with two cups of water until tender. Cool; blend to a smooth purée. Add up to one litre of water, stirring to make a thin mixture. Set aside. Heat the oil in a non-stick *kadai*.
- Add the cumin seeds and, when they begin to change colour, add the spring onion and ginger, and sauté on medium heat for a few seconds. Add the green chillies and continue to sauté for few more seconds.
- Stir in the green gram purée and bring to a boil. Reduce heat, add the lemon juice and simmer, uncovered, for five minutes.Add the vermicelli and simmer for another minute. Add the salt and peppercorns, and stir well. Pour the soup into serving bowls and serve hot.

Makai Aur Shimla Mirch Soup

INGREDIENTS

1½ cups American sweetcorn kernels, boiled

1 medium green capsicum

1 tablespoon oil

1 medium onion, chopped

2 fresh red chillies, diagonally sliced

1 tablespoon cornflour

½ cup skimmed milk

¾ level teaspoon salt

METHOD

- Pierce the capsicum with a fork. Roast the capsicum on an open flame till lightly charred. Dip it in a bowl of water and peel off the charred skin. Remove the seeds and chop roughly. Grind the corn with a little water to a coarse paste.
- Heat the oil in a deep non-stick pan; add the onion and sauté till light brown. Add the ground corn and one cup of water, and stir to mix. Cook for two minutes. Add the capsicum and the red chillies, and cook on low heat for one minute.
- Mix the cornflour with the milk and add to the soup and stir. Cook till the soup thickens slightly. Add water to adjust the consistency. Add the salt. Serve piping hot.

Sodium Content Per Serving: 445 mg

Chilled Cucumber And Buttermilk Soup

Sodium Content Per Serving: 341 mg

INGREDIENTS

2 medium cucumbers, peeled and chopped

3 cups buttermilk (made from skimmed milk yogurt)

½ inch ginger, chopped

1-2 green chillies, chopped

½ teaspoon white pepper powder

6-8 fresh mint leaves + to garnish

2 teaspoons lemon juice

½ level teaspoon salt

METHOD

- Place the chopped cucumber in a blender. Add the ginger, green chillies, white pepper powder and mint leaves, and blend till smooth.
- Add the buttermilk, lemon juice and salt, and blend again.
- Transfer to a serving bowl and place in a refrigerator to chill. Garnish with mint leaves and serve.

Chef's Tip: You can sprinkle a little cumin powder for garnishing.

Pudina Shorba

INGREDIENTS

100 grams fresh mint leaves, chopped roughly

2¼ cups skimmed milk yogurt

1 tablespoon gram flour

2 green chillies, chopped

10 black peppercorns, crushed

1 teaspoon cumin seeds, roasted and powdered

1 inch ginger, chopped

½ level teaspoon salt

METHOD

- Add the gram flour to the yogurt and mix well. Add one cup of water and whisk till smooth.
- Heat the mixture in a non-stick pan. Add the chopped mint, chopped green chillies, crushed peppercorns, roasted cumin powder and chopped ginger. Mix well.
- Add another cup of water and bring to a boil. Lower the heat and simmer for five minutes.
- Strain and bring to a boil once again. Stir in the salt. Remove from heat. Serve immediately.

Sodium Content Per Serving: 321 mg

Tomato Saar

Sodium Content Per Serving: 309 mg

INGREDIENTS

5-6 large tomatoes, roughly chopped

2 tablespoons grated coconut

6 garlic cloves, chopped

1 teaspoon cumin seeds

½ level teaspoon salt

½ teaspoon red chilli powder

1 tablespoon ghee

1 teaspoon mustard seeds

A pinch of asafoetida

8-10 curry leaves

3-4 green chillies, slit

Powdered sugar (optional), as required

1 teaspoon chopped fresh coriander

METHOD

- Grind together the coconut, garlic and cumin seeds.
- Place the tomatoes in a non-stick pan; add one-fourth teaspoon salt and chilli powder and three cups of water and bring it to a boil. Simmer for fifteen minutes and make a purée when cool.
- Heat the pure ghee in a non-stick pan and add the mustard seeds. As they begin to splutter, add the asafoetida and curry leaves. Add the tomato purée and green chillies. Bring to a boil and add coconut paste.
- Cook on low heat for ten minutes. Add the remaining salt and stir. Check the seasoning and add sugar only if needed. Serve hot, garnished with the chopped coriander.

Masoor, Gajar Aur Pumpkin Soup

INGREDIENTS

½ cup split red lentils, soaked

2 medium carrots, sliced

250 grams red pumpkin, chopped

2 teaspoons oil

3 garlic cloves

1 large onion, chopped

7-8 black peppercorns, freshly crushed

¾ cup skimmed milk

¾ level teaspoon salt

METHOD

- Heat the oil in a non-stick pan. Add the garlic, onion, carrots and pumpkin, and sauté for a few minutes. Add one and a half cups of water and the crushed peppercorns and stir.
- Add the lentils and mix well. Cover and cook on medium heat till completely cooked and soft.
- Cool and process in a blender to make a smooth purée. Transfer the purée to a non-stick pan and add the milk. Bring to a boil and stir in the salt. Serve hot.

Sodium Content Per Serving: 485 mg

Tomato Saar

Peppery Corn and Tomato Salad

Peppery Corn And Tomato Salad

Sodium Content Per Serving: 19 mg

INGREDIENTS

15–20 black peppercorns, crushed

1½ cups sweetcorn kernels

3 medium tomatoes, seeded and diced

1 medium yellow capsicum, seeded and diced

2 medium green capsicums, seeded and diced

2 pineapple slices, diced

2 tablespoons lemon juice

2 green chillies, chopped

10-12 fresh mint leaves, chopped

METHOD

- Boil the sweetcorn in water until soft. Drain thoroughly and cool.
- In a bowl, combine the cooled sweetcorn with the capsicums, tomatoes and pineapple. Add the lemon juice, crushed black peppercorns, green chillies and mint, and stir.
- Arrange the salad in a serving dish and chill in the refrigerator before serving.

Fruit Raita

INGREDIENTS

15 green seedless grapes, halved

2 cups skimmed milk yogurt, whisked

1½ teaspoons honey

½ teaspoon roasted cumin powder

1 tablespoon chopped fresh coriander

A quarter pinch of salt

A large pinch of red chilli powder

METHOD

- Place the yogurt in a bowl; add the honey and cumin powder, and stir to mix.
- Add the grapes and chopped coriander, and fold in gently. Place in a refrigerator to chill.
- Sprinkle salt and stir. Sprinkle chilli powder as a garnish and serve.

Sodium Content Per Serving: 168 mg

Citrus Cucumber Salad

Sodium Content Per Serving: 158 mg

INGREDIENTS

1 medium sweet lime, segments removed and halved

5-6 orange segments, halved

1 medium cucumber, peeled and cut into 1-inch strips

1 lettuce leaves

1 tablespoon lemon juice

½ tablespoon salad oil

A generous pinch of red chilli flakes

4-5 fresh mint leaves

¼ level teaspoon salt

½ medium carrot, cut into thin strips

1 small tomato, quartered and sliced

METHOD

- Trim the lettuce leaves, wash under running water and soak in chilled water, to keep them fresh and crisp.
- In a bowl, mix together the lemon juice, salad oil, red chilli flakes and mint leaves. Add salt and whisk well.
- Drain the lettuce leaves and tear them into bite-size pieces. Arrange a bed of lettuce leaves on a serving dish. Drizzle one-fourth of the dressing over the leaves.
- Combine the sweet lime and orange segments, cucumber, carrot and tomato in a bowl.
- Add the remaining dressing, toss to mix and spoon onto the bed of lettuce. Serve immediately.

Kosumali

Sodium Content
Per Serving: 301 mg

INGREDIENTS

½ cup skinless split green gram

⅔ cup sprouted green gram

1 medium cucumber, seeded and chopped

2 green chillies, chopped

1 tablespoon chopped fresh coriander

1 tablespoon lemon juice

½ level teaspoon salt

2 teaspoons oil

1 teaspoon mustard seeds

8–10 curry leaves

1 tablespoon grated coconut

METHOD

- Soak the green gram in one cup water for thirty minutes. Drain and place in a non-stick pan. Add one cup of water and cook until the *dal* is just done. Drain again and set aside to cool.
- Boil the gram sprouts until just cooked. Drain and set aside.
- In a large bowl, mix together the cooked *dal* and sprouts, cucumber, chillies and chopped coriander. Add the lemon juice and salt, and mix well.
- Heat the oil in a non-stick pan. Add the mustard seeds, and when they splutter, add the curry leaves. Add the seasoning to the *dal* mixture and stir well.
- Garnish with the grated coconut and serve at room temperature.

Moong-Moth Ka Anokha Salad

Sodium Content Per Serving: 335 mg

INGREDIENTS

½ cup sprouted green gram

½ cup sprouted brown gram

½ level teaspoon salt

1 green chilli, finely chopped

1 medium onion, cut into ½-inch cubes and layers separated

1 medium green capsicum, cut into ½-inch cubes

1 medium cucumber, cut into ½-inch cubes

2 medium tomatoes, cut into ½-inch pieces

¼ medium apple, thinly sliced

5-6 freshly crushed black peppercorns

1 tablespoon lemon juice

METHOD

- Place the sprouted green gram and sprouted brown gram in two separate microwave-safe bowls.
- Add the salt and half a cup of water to each bowl and cook in a microwave oven for two minutes on HIGH (100%). Drain and transfer to a deep bowl.
- Add the green chill, onion, capsicum, cucumber, tomatoes and apple, and mix.
- Add the peppercorns and lemon juice, and mix. Chill in a refrigerator before serving.

Phalon Ka Kachumber

Sodium Content Per Serving: 391 mg

INGREDIENTS

1 medium apple

2 medium oranges

12-15 seedless green grapes, halved

2 medium tomatoes, seeded and sliced thinly

1 medium cucumber, halved vertically and sliced thinly

1 medium green capsicum, seeded and sliced thinly

2 spring onions, sliced thinly

2 tablespoons lemon juice

½ cup fresh coriander, chopped

A few sprigs of fresh mint, chopped

2 green chillies, chopped

½ level teaspoon black salt

METHOD

- Wash and core the apple, cut into halves and slice thinly. Coat with one tablespoon of lemon juice immediately to prevent discolouration.
- Peel the oranges and separate the segments. Remove the seeds and halve each segment.
- Mix together the chopped coriander and mint, the green chillies, black salt and remaining lemon juice to make a dressing.
- Toss the prepared fruit and vegetable in the dressing.
- Place in a refrigerator and serve chilled.

Lapsi Aur Shimla Mirch Salad

Sodium Content Per Serving: 310 mg

INGREDIENTS

200 grams broken wheat

2 medium red capsicums

1 medium yellow capsicum

1 medium onion, sliced

4 garlic cloves, thinly sliced

2 medium tomatoes, seeded and diced

1 tablespoon chopped fresh coriander

½ level teaspoon salt

Ground white pepper to taste

A pinch of sugar

1 tablespoon lemon juice

4 tablespoons finely chopped fresh mint

A few iceberg lettuce leaves

METHOD

- Soak the broken wheat in water for fifteen to twenty minutes. Drain.
- Pierce each capsicum with a fork. Roast the capsicum on an open flame till lightly charred. Dip it in a bowl of water and peel off the charred skin. Remove the seeds and cut into small pieces.
- Place the soaked wheat in a salad bowl, and stir in the onion and garlic.
- Stir in the chopped capsicum, tomatoes and chopped coriander; add the salt, white pepper powder and sugar, and mix.
- Add the lemon juice and chopped mint.
- Tear the iceberg lettuce and add to the salad. Toss well and serve.

Slimmers' Salad In No-Oil Dressing

Sodium Content Per Serving: 363 mg

INGREDIENTS

1 medium head of iceberg lettuce

2 oranges, separated into segments and halved

A few sprigs of fresh mint leaves

10-12 black peppercorns

1 teaspoon mustard seeds

4 garlic cloves

3 tablespoons lemon juice

2 teaspoons malt vinegar

1 medium onion, quartered and layers separated

¼ small watermelon, seeded and cubed

1 medium cucumber, seeded and cubed

2 medium tomatoes, seeded cubed

1 celery stalk, chopped

1 medium green capsicum, diced

2 spring onions, cut into 1-inch pieces

½ level teaspoon salt

METHOD

- Tear the lettuce into bite-sized pieces and soak in ice-cold water to keep them crisp.
- Reserve some mint leaves for garnishing and chop the rest.
- Crush the peppercorns, mustard seeds and garlic with lemon juice with a mortar and pestle. Stir in the malt vinegar.
- In a bowl, mix all the fruit, vegetables and chopped mint leaves.
- Add the dressing and toss well. Add the salt and toss again.
- Serve the salad on a bed of crisp lettuce, garnished with reserved mint leaves.

Ambe Dal

Sodium Content Per Serving: 357 mg

INGREDIENTS

1 small unripe green mango, grated

1½ cups split Bengal gram

½ teaspoon cumin seeds

2 green chillies

½ teaspoon grated jaggery

1 teaspoon oil

A generous pinch of asafoetida

½ teaspoon mustard seeds

2 dried red chillies, broken into large bits

½ teaspoon turmeric powder

1 tablespoon grated coconut (optional)

½ level teaspoon salt

2 tablespoons chopped fresh coriander

METHOD

- Soak the split gram in four cups of water for at least four hours. Drain
- Pound the cumin seeds and green chillies with a mortar and pestle. Add the jaggery and the drained split gram and pound into a coarse mixture.
- Heat the oil in a non stick pan; add the asafoetida and mustard seeds. When the seeds begin to splutter, add the red chillies and turmeric powder. Stir and take the pan off the heat and let it cool to room temperature.
- Transfer the *dal* mixture to a bowl. Add the grated mango and coconut, and mix well. Add the seasoning to the *dal* mixture and mix well. Sprinkle the salt and toss to mix.
- Garnish with the chopped coriander and serve immediately.

Note: This dish has a shelf life of only three to four hours, so it should be consumed immediately.

Nutritious Soya Kababs

Sodium Content Per Serving: 439 mg

INGREDIENTS

2 cups soya chunks (nuggets), soaked and drained

1 large onion, finely chopped

2 green chillies, finely chopped

1 teaspoon coriander powder

¾ level teaspoon salt

1 teaspoon cumin powder

½ teaspoon red chilli powder

1 inch ginger, grated

¼ teaspoon dried mango powder

150 grams bean curd (tofu), grated

½ cup beaten rice, soaked and mashed

1 teaspoon *garam masala* powder

1 tablespoon chopped fresh coriander

Oil for brushing

METHOD

- Blend together the soya chunks, onion, green chillies, coriander powder, salt, cumin powder, chilli powder, ginger and dried mango powder in a blender.
- Add the bean curd and continue to blend for two more minutes.
- Transfer the mixture to a bowl, add the mashed beaten rice, *garam masala* powder and chopped coriander, and mix well.
- Preheat an oven to 180°C/350°F/Gas Mark 4.
- Divide the mixture into sixteen equal portions and shape them into flat round *kababs*.
- Grease a baking tray with oil. Gently place the *kababs* on the tray and lightly brush with oil.
- Bake for fifteen minutes, turn over the *kababs* and bake on the other side for seven to eight minutes. Serve hot.

Baked Samosa

Sodium Content Per Serving: 305 mg

INGREDIENTS

Pastry

1 cup wholewheat flour

½ teaspoon carom seeds

¼ level teaspoon salt

Filling

1 teaspoon cumin seeds

½ inch piece ginger, chopped

2 green chillies, chopped

2 medium potatoes, cut into small pieces

2 tablespoons fresh green peas

½ teaspoon red chilli powder

½ teaspoon dried mango powder

½ teaspoon *garam masala* powder

¼ level teaspoon salt

2 tablespoons chopped fresh coriander

METHOD

- Mix together all the ingredients for the pastry. Add water and knead to a smooth, stiff dough. Rest the dough, covered with a damp cloth, for ten to fifteen minutes.
- For the filling, heat a non-stick pan and lightly roast the cumin seeds. Add the ginger, green chillies, potatoes and green peas, and stir.
- Add the chilli powder, dried mango powder, *garam masala* powder and salt, and stir well to mix.
- Sprinkle over a little water and cook, covered, for ten to twelve minutes. Add the chopped coriander and mix. Remove from heat and leave to cool. Divide into eight equal portions.
- Preheat an oven to 200°C/400°F/Gas Mark 6.
- Divide the dough into four equal portions and roll them into balls. Roll out the balls into oval puri. Cut each one in half and moisten the edges with water. Shape each half into a cone and stuff it with the potato-pea filling. Press the edges well to seal.
- Arrange the samose on a baking tray and bake in the oven at 180°C/350°F/Gas Mark 4 for twenty to twenty-five minutes, turning them every five minutes. Serve hot

Hot And Sour Idli

Sodium Content Per Serving: 307 mg

INGREDIENTS

1 cup split pigeon peas

1 cup rice

6 dried red chillies

2 tablespoons tamarind pulp

A large pinch of asafoetida

½ teaspoon turmeric powder

½ level teaspoon salt

1 tablespoon grated jaggery

2 finely chopped small onions

METHOD

- Wash and soak the split pigeon peas and the rice separately in three cups of water each for four to six hours.
- Drain and grind the split pigeon peas to a smooth paste and the rice to a coarse paste. Mix them together thoroughly. Set aside for four or five hours to ferment.
- Grind the red chillies and tamarind to a fine paste.
- Add the asafoetida, turmeric powder, salt and red chilli-tamarind paste to the batter and mix well. Dissolve jaggery in a little water and stir into the batter.
- Heat a little water in a steamer or pressure cooker. Grease the *idli* moulds.
- Pour the batter into the moulds, sprinkle the onions on top and steam for about fifteen minutes or till done.
- Serve hot with chutney of your choice.

Chef's Tip: These *idli* are quite different from traditional *idli* made from rice and skinless split black gram, however they taste equally good. As these *idli* have tamarind, chillies and jaggery, you can eat them as an any-time snack.

Kachche Kele Ki Tikki

Sodium Content
Per Serving: 302 mg

INGREDIENTS

3 medium unripe bananas

¼ cup boiled green peas

2 green chillies, chopped

1 tablespoon chopped fresh coriander

¼ teaspoon dried mango powder

½ teaspoon *garam masala* powder

½ level teaspoon salt

A pinch of asafoetida

¼ teaspoon red chilli powder

2 tablespoons oil for shallow-frying

METHOD

- Cut each unripe banana into three pieces without peeling them. Steam them in a steamer for ten minutes. Cool, peel and grate the bananas.
- Grind the green peas, green chillies and chopped coriander to a coarse mixture. Add to the grated bananas. Add the dried mango powder, *garam masala* powder, salt, asafoetida, chilli powder, and mix well.
- Divide into eight equal portions. Grease your palms and shape each portion into a round tikki at least half inch thick.
- Heat the oil in a non-stick pan. Place five to six tikki at a time in the pan and shallow-fry for three to four minutes or till the underside is light golden brown. Turn them over and continue to cook for three to four minutes longer or till the other side is equally light golden.
- Serve hot.

Methi-Gajar Muthia

Sodium Content Per Serving: 491 mg

INGREDIENTS

½ cup fresh fenugreek leaves, finely chopped

2 small carrots, grated

2½ cups coarse wholewheat flour

¾ cup gram flour

¾ level teaspoon salt

1 teaspoon ginger-garlic paste

¼ teaspoon turmeric powder

¾ teaspoon red chilli powder

¼ teaspoon green chilli paste

¼ teaspoon garam *masala* powder

1 tablespoon lemon juice

1 teaspoon grated jaggery

2 tablespoons skimmed milk yogurt

1 tablespoon sesame seeds, roasted

METHOD

- Place the flour in a bowl. Add the chopped fenugreek, carrot, gram flour, salt, ginger-garlic paste, turmeric powder, chilli powder, green chilli paste, *garam masala* powder, lemon juice, jaggery, yogurt and sesame seeds.
- Mix everything well. Add a little water and knead into a stiff dough. Divide the dough into twelve equal portions and shape into small rolls (*muthia*).
- Heat some water in a steamer or pan.
- Place the *muthia* in perforated plates and steam, covered, for twenty to twenty-five minutes.
- Serve hot.

Bhelpuri With Sprouts

Sodium Content Per Serving: 324 mg

INGREDIENTS

½ cup green gram sprouts, blanched

2 cups puffed rice

1 small potato, boiled, peeled and diced

1 small unripe mango, chopped

1 medium onion, chopped

½ level teaspoon salt

¼ teaspoon red chilli powder

1 tablespoon chopped fresh coriander

2-3 green chillies, chopped

½ cup Date And Tamarind Chutney (page 103)

Red Chilli-Garlic Chutney, as required

2 tablespoons nylon sev

METHOD

- Place the potato in a bowl; add the mango, onion, sprouted green gram, reserving some for garnishing, salt, chilli powder, chopped coriander, green chillies date and tamarind chutney and mix.
- Add the puffed rice and red chilli-garlic chutney and mix.
- Serve immediately topped with the remaining sprouts and sev.

Khandvi

INGREDIENTS

1 cup gram flour

1 inch ginger, chopped

2 green chillies, broken into two

½ cup skimmed milk yogurt

METHOD

- Sift the gram flour into a deep bowl and set aside.
- Place the ginger and chillies in a blender with one teaspoon of water and grind to a smooth paste. Place the yogurt in a small bowl and add half a cup of water. Whisk together to make buttermilk. Add the citric acid and stir to dissolve. Stir in one and a quarter cups of water. Set aside.

Sodium Content Per Serving: 329 mg

A generous pinch of citric acid

½ level teaspoon salt

½ teaspoon turmeric powder

1 tablespoon lemon juice

3 teaspoons oil

A pinch of asafoetida

1 teaspoon mustard seeds

2 tablespoons chopped fresh coriander

- Add the ginger-chilli paste to the gram flour in the bowl along with the salt, turmeric, lemon juice, buttermilk, two teaspoons of oil and asafoetida. Whisk, to make a smooth batter.
- Pour the gram flour mixture into a large non-stick pan. Cook on medium heat for seven to eight minutes, stirring continuously. Lower the heat and continue to cook, stirring continuously, for eight to ten minutes, or till the mixture becomes thick.
- To check if the batter is of the right consistency, take about a half a teaspoonful and spread it thinly on the back of a clean dry *thali*. Allow it to cool for one minute. Lift it off the surface by rolling it like a Swiss roll. The batter should come off cleanly it is cooked.
- Remove the pan from heat and working quickly, spread half the cooked gram flour mixture over the back of one stainless steel *thali* and remaining half over the back of another *thali*, as thinly as possible while the batter is still hot. The batter should spread easily.
- Set aside to cool. Cut into two-inch wide strips and roll up tightly. Place each roll gently in a serving dish.
- Place a small non-stick pan over medium heat and pour in one teaspoon of oil and add the mustard seeds When they splutter, pour the seasoning over the rolls.
- Sprinkle the chopped coriander over the rolls and serve immediately.

Chef's Tip: Making *khandvi* is an art. It takes some practice to cook the batter to the right consistency. Try out a small portion first. *Khandvi* can be stored in a refrigerator for a maximum of six hours. It is best eaten immediately.

Murmura Chiwda

Sodium Content Per Serving: 147 mg

INGREDIENTS

3 cups puffed rice

1 teaspoon oil

¼ teaspoon mustard seeds

2 green chillies, slit

1 tablespoon roasted split Bengal gram

1 tablespoon unsalted peanuts, slightly crushed

10–15 curry leaves

¼ teaspoon turmeric powder

¼ level teaspoon salt

METHOD

- Heat the oil in a deep non-stick *kadai*. Add the mustard seeds, green chillies, roasted split Bengal gram, peanuts and curry leaves, and sauté for two minutes.
- Add the turmeric powder, puffed rice and salt. Toss well to mix. Roast on low heat, tossing frequently till the puffed rice is crisp.
- Cool completely and store in an airtight tin.

Cornflakes Ki Chaat

INGREDIENTS

2 cups cornflakes

4 tablespoons cucumber, seeded and chopped

1 small potato, boiled and cut into cubes

2 small tomatoes, chopped

2 green chillies, chopped

¼ teaspoon roasted cumin powder

¼ teaspoon red chilli powder

½ level teaspoon salt

1 teaspoon chopped fresh coriander

METHOD

- Squeeze out the excess water from the cucumber and mix with the potato, tomatoes and green chillies in a bowl.
- Add the roasted cumin powder, chilli powder and salt and mix well.
- Add the cornflakes and toss to mix.
- Serve, garnished with chopped coriander.

Sodium Content Per Serving: 399 mg

Cornflakes Ki Chaat

Prawn Varuval

Sodium Content
Per Serving: 349 mg

INGREDIENTS

16 medium prawns, shelled and deveined

1 inch ginger

12 garlic cloves

2 tablespoons tamarind pulp

1½ teaspoons roasted cumin powder

1 tablespoon red chilli powder

½ teaspoon turmeric powder

½ level teaspoon salt

4 tablespoons rice flour

1½ tablespoons oil

1½ tablespoons lemon juice

METHOD

- Grind the ginger and garlic to a fine paste and combine with the tamarind pulp, cumin powder, chilli powder, turmeric powder, salt and rice flour in a bowl.
- Stir half a tablespoon of oil into the mixture. Add the prawn, mix well and leave to marinate for at least two hours, preferably in a refrigerator.
- Heat the remaining oil in a non-stick pan; add the marinated prawns with the marinade and cook for one minute on a high heat.
- Turn the prawns over and cook for another minute. Reduce the heat and cook for another two to three minutes, turning the prawns occasionally to ensure they cook evenly.
- Remove the prawns from the pan and drain on absorbent paper. Sprinkle with the lemon juice and serve.

Moong Dal Uttapam

Sodium Content Per Serving: 305 mg

INGREDIENTS

1 cup skinless split green gram, soaked

½ level teaspoon salt

¼ teaspoon turmeric powder

Cow's milk ghee for shallow-frying

Topping

1 large green capsicum, seeded and diced

1 small tomato, seeded and diced

1 small onion, diced

4-5 green chillies, chopped (optional)

METHOD

- Drain the green gram and grind it to a coarse paste.
- Transfer into a bowl and add salt and turmeric powder. Mix well and set aside.
- In a separate bowl, mix together the capsicum, tomato, onion and green chillies.
- Heat a non-stick pan and pour a small ladleful of the *dal* batter and spread it evenly into a round, taking care that it is not too thin. Drizzle a little of the ghee around the sides.
- Spread some of the topping over it.
- Cook for a minute and turn the pancake over. Drizzle a little ghee around the sides and cook the other side till golden.
- Serve hot.

Chicken Seekh Kabab

Sodium Content Per Serving: 530 mg

INGREDIENTS

500 grams finely minced chicken breast

2 green chillies, finely chopped

1 medium onion, finely chopped

1 inch ginger, finely chopped

4 garlic cloves, finely chopped

½ teaspoon *garam masala* powder

½ teaspoon white pepper powder

2 tablespoons chopped fresh coriander

1 tablespoon lemon juice

¾ level teaspoon rock salt

1 teaspoon oil

METHOD

- In a bowl, mix together the minced chicken, green chillies, onion, ginger, garlic, *garam masala* powder, white pepper powder, chopped coriander, lemon juice and rock salt.
- Alternatively, grind boneless chicken together with the green chillies, onion, ginger and garlic.
- Add the remaining ingredients and mix. For each kabab wet your hands, take a little chicken mixture and shape it around a satay stick. Press firmly.
- Heat a non-stick *tawa* and drizzle the oil on it. Place the *kababs* on the *tawa*. Cook, turning from time to time, so that they roast evenly on all sides.
- Serve immediately.

Peshawari Tangdi Kabab

Sodium Content Per Serving: 311 mg

INGREDIENTS

8 chicken drumsticks

2 teaspoons oil

1 lemon, cut into wedges

First Marinade

2 tablespoons ginger-garlic paste

2 tablespoons lemon juice

1 teaspoon oil

Second Marinade

½ cup drained (hung) skimmed milk yogurt

1 tablespoon garlic paste

1 tablespoon ginger paste

½ level teaspoon salt

2 teaspoons red chilli powder

1 teaspoon *garam masala* powder

1 teaspoon mustard oil

1 teaspoon lemon rind

METHOD

- Make light incisions on the chicken legs. Mix together the ginger-garlic paste, lemon juice and oil, and rub onto the chicken legs and set aside for one hour in the refrigerator.
- For the second marinade, mix together the drained yogurt, garlic paste, ginger paste, salt, chilli powder, *garam masala* powder and mustard oil in a bowl and rub well onto the chicken drumsticks. Add the lemon rind, mix well and set aside for two hours in the refrigerator.
- Preheat an oven to 200°C/400°F/Gas Mark 6..
- Place the chicken on a baking tray and cook in the preheated for twenty minutes.
- Drizzle the oil over the chicken, turn the pieces over and cook for five to eight minutes longer. Serve hot with lemon wedges.

Pudina Kali Mirch Rawas Tikka

Sodium Content Per Serving: 377 mg

INGREDIENTS

20-25 fresh mint leaves, coarsely chopped

4-5 tablespoons crushed black peppercorns

500 grams Indian salmon (*rawas*) fillets, cut into 1½-inch cubes

2 teaspoons oil

3 tablespoons gram flour

2 tablespoons lemon juice

½ level teaspoon salt

¼ teaspoon turmeric powder

¼ cup skimmed milk yogurt

1 teaspoon carom seeds

A pinch of *garam masala* powder

1 teaspoon garlic paste

1 teaspoon ginger paste

METHOD

- Brush a non-stick pan with a little oil. Add the gram flour and roast for three to four minutes.
- Add the lemon juice, salt and turmeric powder to the fish cubes and marinate for about fifteen minutes.
- Mix together the mint leaves, yogurt, roasted gram flour, carom seeds, *garam masala* powder, garlic paste and ginger paste. Add the fish cubes and mix. Set aside to marinate for half an hour.
- Thread the fish cubes close to each other onto skewers. This will help to retain their moisture.
- Roll the skewers in the crushed black peppercorns and cook on the barbecue, rotating the skewers and basting with the remaining oil a few times, till the fish is completely cooked.
- Serve hot.

Mushroom Tikki

Sodium Content Per Serving: 313 mg

INGREDIENTS

12-15 fresh button mushrooms

2-3 teaspoons oil

3 medium onions, chopped

2 medium potatoes, boiled and mashed

2-3 green chillies, chopped

1 tablespoon chopped fresh coriander

½ level teaspoon salt

1 cup semolina

METHOD

- Boil the mushrooms in water for about ten minutes. Drain and chop finely.
- Heat one teaspoon oil in a non-stick pan. Add the onions and sauté till soft and translucent. Add the mushrooms and sauté till all the moisture evaporates. Add the green chillies and mix.
- Place the potatoes in a bowl. Add the mushroom mixture to the potatoes and mix well. Add the chopped coriander and salt, and mix.
- Heat a non-stick pan. Brush with a little oil or spray with a little oil.
- Place the semolina in a plate. Shape the mushroom mixture into eight tikki. Roll in the semolina, press slightly and fry till golden brown.
- Serve hot.

Baked Shankerpali

Sodium Content Per Serving: 325 mg

INGREDIENTS

½ cup wholewheat flour

½ cup refined flour

3-4 garlic cloves, crushed

½ level teaspoon salt

½ teaspoon red chilli powder

½ teaspoon roasted cumin powder

½ cup thick freshly made tomato purée

2 tablespoons cow's milk ghee

METHOD

- Preheat an oven to 170°C/325°F/Gas Mark 3. Line a baking tray with a silicon baking sheet.
- Place the wholewheat flour and refined flour in a bowl. Add the crushed garlic, salt, chilli powder, cumin powder, tomato purée and ghee, and mix. Knead into a medium soft dough. Cover the dough with a damp cloth and rest it for fifteen minutes.
- Roll out into a round disc taking care not to roll it too thin.
- Cut into small triangles. Separate the pieces and arrange them on the silicon lined baking tray. Bake for ten to fifteen minutes. Check to see if they are crisp. If not, bake for five minutes longer.
- Remove from the oven and set aside to cool to room temperature.
- Store in an airtight container.

Besan-Methi Frankie

Sodium Content Per Serving: 327 mg

INGREDIENTS

½ cup gram flour

¾ cup wholewheat flour + for dusting

1 cup chopped fresh fenugreek leaves

4 green chillies, chopped

¼ teaspoon turmeric powder

¼ teaspoon carom seeds

1 tablespoon skimmed milk yogurt

¼ level teaspoon salt

2 tablespoons unsalted mint chutney (see below)

Stuffing

1 teaspoon oil

2 medium tomatoes, seeded and chopped

2 green chillies, chopped

1 cup bean sprouts

¼ teaspoon turmeric powder

¼ teaspoon red chilli powder

¼ level teaspoon salt

1 teaspoon lemon juice

METHOD

- Mix together the two flours, fenugreek leaves, green chillies, turmeric powder, carom seeds, yogurt and salt. Add enough water to knead into a semi-soft dough. Cover the dough with a damp cloth and rest for about fifteen minutes.
- For the stuffing, heat the oil in a non-stick pan, add the tomatoes and sauté for two minutes. Add the green chillies and bean sprouts and continue to sauté for thirty seconds. Stir in the turmeric powder, chilli powder, and salt. Sprinkle some water, cover and cook till bean sprouts are done. Add the lemon juice and sauté for one minute. Remove from heat and set aside.
- Divide the dough into eight equal portions and roll into balls. Dust with a little wholewheat flour, and roll out into a *roti* roughly six-inch in diameter.
- Heat a non-stick *tawa* and cook the *roti* on both sides, until evenly done. To prepare a frankie, place a *roti* on a flat work surface and spread a teaspoon of green chutney all over. Spoon some of the stuffing on one side of the *roti*, and roll up.
- Prepare the rest of the frankies in the same way, wrapping them up in aluminium foil. Serve immediately.

Chef's Tip: To make the chutney, grind together 1 cup roughly chopped fresh mint leaves, 2 chopped green chillies, 2 teaspoons lemon juice, ¼ teaspoon crushed black peppercorns, ½ inch ginger to make a paste.

Brown Poha

Sodium Content Per Serving: 477 mg

INGREDIENTS

250 grams beaten brown rice

1 tablespoon oil

1 teaspoon mustard seeds

10–12 curry leaves

2 medium onions, chopped

2 green chillies, slit and seeded

1 tablespoon roasted unsalted peanuts (optional)

¼ teaspoon turmeric powder

½ level teaspoon salt

2 tablespoons lightly cooked green peas

1 tablespoon lemon juice

3 tablespoons chopped fresh coriander

METHOD

- Soak the beaten rice in water for fifteen to twenty minutes. Drain.
- Heat the oil in a non-stick pan. Add the mustard seeds, curry leaves, onions and chillies, and sauté for two minutes.
- Stir in the roasted peanuts and turmeric powder, and mix. Stir in the drained beaten rice and salt. Cook for two to three minutes.
- Add the peas and lemon juice, and mix again.
- Garnish with the chopped coriander and serve hot.

Aluchi Patal Bhaji

Sodium Content Per Serving: 300 mg

INGREDIENTS

6 colocasia leaves, shredded

¼ cup Bengal gram, soaked

3 tablespoons Tamarind Pulp (page 103)

1 tablespoon oil

½ teaspoon mustard seeds

5-6 curry leaves

A generous pinch of asafoetida

¼ teaspoon fenugreek seeds

4 garlic cloves, finely chopped

3 green chillies, finely chopped

¼ teaspoon turmeric powder

3 tablespoons gram flour

½ level teaspoon salt

1 tablespoon raw peanuts

1 tablespoon grated jaggery

1 tablespoon grated coconut

METHOD

- Cook the colocasia leaves with the tamarind pulp and Bengal gram in four cups of water in a non-stick pan till soft.
- Heat the oil in a non-stick pan. Add the mustard seeds, curry leaves, asafoetida, fenugreek seeds, garlic, and sauté for one minute. Add the green chillies and turmeric powder, and sauté for half a minute. Add the gram flour and sauté for a minute.
- Add the cooked colocasia-Bengal gram mixture, salt and half a cup of water, if required.
- Add the peanuts and adjust the consistency of the gravy. Cook for five minutes and add the grated jaggery. Bring to a boil again. Add the grated coconut and some more water if required, and cook on medium heat for half an hour, stirring occasionally.
- Serve hot.

Tindora Nu Shaak

Sodium Content Per Serving: 315 mg

INGREDIENTS

300 grams ivy gourd, thinly sliced

1 tablespoon oil

¼ teaspoon mustard seeds

A pinch of asafoetida

1 teaspoon coriander powder

1 teaspoon roasted cumin powder

¼ teaspoon turmeric powder

½ level teaspoon salt

METHOD

- Heat the oil in a non-stick *kadai*; add the mustard seeds and asafoetida. When the seeds begin to splutter, add the sliced gourds and sauté on low heat for five to seven minutes.
- Add all the spices and the salt and cook on a high heat for two to three minutes.
- Remove from heat when crisp.

Bharli Mirchi

Sodium Content Per Serving: 293 mg

INGREDIENTS

8 large Bhavnagri green chillies

½ level teaspoon salt

3 teaspoons oil

½ teaspoon mustard seeds

A pinch of asafoetida

1 teaspoon turmeric powder

3 tablespoons grated coconut

¾ teaspoon red chilli powder

½ teaspoon fennel powder

¼ teaspoon cumin powder

¼ teaspoon coriander powder

1 tablespoon grated unripe mango

2 tablespoons chopped fresh coriander

METHOD

- Slit the green chillies and remove the seeds. Apply one-fourth teaspoon of salt and set aside for thirty minutes. Wash and drain well.
- Heat one teaspoon oil in a non-stick pan and add the mustard seeds. When they splutter add the asafoetida and turmeric powder. Add the coconut and sauté till lightly coloured.
- Add the chilli powder, fennel powder, cumin powder, coriander powder, and remaining salt. Sauté till well mixed and dry. Add the mango and continue to sauté.
- Add the chopped coriander, mix well, remove from heat and set aside to cool.
- Stuff the mixture into chillies and set aside.
- Heat the remaining oil in a non-stick frying pan. Place the chillies in the pan, cover and cook for two to three minutes. Turn the chillies over, cover and continue to cook for two to three minutes longer or till both sides are evenly cooked.
- Remove and serve hot.

Cabbage-Chana Dal

Sodium Content Per Serving: 299 mg

INGREDIENTS

1 medium cabbage, shredded

¼ cup split Bengal gram, soaked

1 teaspoon mustard seeds

10-12 curry leaves

4 dried red chillies

1 inch ginger, chopped

½ teaspoon turmeric powder

½ level teaspoon salt

½ teaspoon *garam masala* powder

1 tablespoon chopped fresh coriander

METHOD

- Drain and cook the Bengal gram in approximately one cup of water till just tender. Drain and set aside.
- Heat a non-stick pan; add the mustard seeds and dry-roast for half a minute. Add the curry leaves and red chillies, and dry-roast for another half minute. Add the ginger and cook for a minute on low heat.
- Add the cabbage and cook till soft. Add the turmeric powder and salt, and stir. Add the cooked Bengal gram and mix well. Cook for two minutes. Add *garam masala* powder and mix.
- Garnish with chopped coriander and serve hot.

Khumb Shaslik

Sodium Content Per Serving: 304 mg

INGREDIENTS

10-12 large fresh button mushrooms

1 medium onion, cut into 1½-inch pieces, layers separated

2 medium tomatoes, seeded and cut into 1½-inch pieces

2 medium green capsicums, cut into 1½-inch pieces

2 tablespoons drained (hung) skimmed yogurt

½ tablespoon Kashmiri red chilli powder

1 teaspoon *garam masala* powder

1 teaspoon crushed dried fenugreek leaves

2 teaspoons ginger paste

2 teaspoons garlic paste

½ level teaspoon salt

2 teaspoons cow's milk ghee

METHOD

- Mix together the drained yogurt, chilli powder, *garam masala* powder, dried fenugreek leaves, ginger paste, garlic paste and salt, and mix well.
- Cut the stems of the mushrooms and add to the yogurt mixture along with the onion, tomatoes and green capsicum. Marinate for half an hour.
- Thread them onto skewers in the following order – onion, mushroom, green capsicum and tomato. Repeat once ending with a piece of onion.
- Place the skewers on the barbecue and roast, basting with ghee from time to time. Rotate the skewers a few times so that the vegetables cook evenly on al sides.
- Serve hot.

Lauki-Moong Dal

Sodium Content
Per Serving: 302 mg

INGREDIENTS

4-inch piece bottle gourd, peeled and diced

1 cup skinless split green gram, soaked

½ level teaspoon salt

¼ teaspoon turmeric powder

½ inch ginger, chopped

8-10 fresh mint leaves

1 teaspoon cow's milk ghee

A large pinch of asafoetida

1 teaspoon cumin seeds

½ inch cinnamon

6-8 curry leaves

1½ tablespoons lemon juice

METHOD

- Cook the green gram with four cups of water, salt, the turmeric powder and ginger in a deep non-stick pan till almost tender.
- Add the bottle gourd and cook for a few minutes. Add the mint leaves and continue to cook till the *dal* and bottle gourd are completely soft.
- Heat the ghee in a small non-stick pan. Add the asafoetida, cumin seeds, cinnamon and curry leaves, and sauté till fragrant. Add to the *dal* and mix.
- Add the lemon juice and serve hot.

Drumstick Curry

Sodium Content Per Serving: 299 mg

INGREDIENTS

4 drumsticks, peeled and cut into 2-inch pieces

1 tablespoon oil

20 curry leaves

2 medium onions, sliced

1 teaspoon curry powder

1 cup thin low-fat coconut milk

½ level teaspoon salt

4 green chillies, slit

1½ tablespoons tamarind pulp

1 teaspoon chopped fresh coriander

METHOD

- Heat the oil in a deep non-stick pan, add the curry leaves and onions, and sauté till lightly browned.
- Add the drumsticks and stir. Add the curry powder and stir again.
- Add the coconut milk, salt and green chillies. Stir and add half a cup of water. Cover and cook till the drumsticks are tender and soft.
- Add the tamarind pulp and mix. Add the chopped coriander and serve hot.

Beans Poriyal

Sodium Content Per Serving: 291 mg

INGREDIENTS

250 grams French beans, cut into ¼-inch pieces

1 tablespoon oil

½ teaspoon mustard seeds

1 teaspoon skinless split black gram

A pinch of asafoetida

2 dried red chillies, broken into large bits

8-10 curry leaves

½ level teaspoon salt

1 tablespoon grated coconut

METHOD

- Heat the oil in a medium-sized non-stick pan on medium heat. Add the mustard seeds and split black gram and sauté till the mustard splutters and the gram turns light brown.
- Add the asafoetida and red chillies, and sauté for half a minute.
- Add the French beans, curry leaves and salt. Add two tablespoons of water and cook for ten to fifteen minutes, or till the beans are cooked.
- Garnish with the coconut and serve hot.

Mixed Sprout Ussal

Sodium Content Per Serving: 300 mg

INGREDIENTS

1 cup mixed sprouts (such as *moong*, *matki,* and *chana*)

½ teaspoon mustard seeds

6–8 curry leaves

2 medium onions, chopped

½ teaspoon turmeric powder

½ teaspoon red chilli powder

1 teaspoon *goda masala*

1 teaspoon grated jaggery

½ level teaspoon salt

Masala Paste

6–7 garlic cloves

3–4 green chillies, chopped

1 teaspoon cumin seeds, roasted

1 tablespoon grated fresh coconut

METHOD

- For the *masala* paste, grind together the garlic, green chillies, cumin seeds and grated coconut to make a smooth paste. Set aside.
- Heat a non-stick pan and add the mustard seeds. When they splutter add the curry leaves and onions, and dry-roast, stirring continuously, till the onions turn light golden.
- Stir in the paste and cook on a medium heat for three to four minutes.
- Add the turmeric powder, chilli powder, *goda masala*, jaggery and salt, and stir well.
- Add the sprouts to the pan, mix well, and add just enough water to cover. Bring to a boil and cook on medium heat, stirring occasionally, until the sprouts are tender. Serve hot.

Palak-Baby Corn

Sodium Content Per Serving: 347 mg

INGREDIENTS

125 grams spinach, blanched and puréed

12-16 pieces of baby corn, cut into small pieces

1 tablespoon oil

5-6 garlic cloves, sliced

¼ teaspoon asafoetida

2 green chillies, chopped

½ teaspoon *garam masala* powder

½ level teaspoon salt

½ tablespoon lemon juice

2 tablespoons chopped fresh coriander

METHOD

- Heat the oil in a non-stick *kadai*; add the garlic and sauté until golden brown. Add the asafoetida and chillies, and sauté for ten seconds.
- Add the baby corn; sauté for two minutes and add the spinach purée, *garam masala* powder and salt. Sauté for two minutes longer.
- Sprinkle the lemon juice and garnish with the fresh coriander.

Pumpkin Foogath

Sodium Content
Per Serving: 299 mg

INGREDIENTS

700 grams red pumpkin, cut into 1-inch cubes

1 tablespoon oil

¼ teaspoon mustard seeds

10-12 curry leaves

A pinch of asafoetida

½ teaspoon turmeric powder

2 medium onions, chopped

3 green chillies, chopped

½ level teaspoon salt

1 tablespoon lemon juice

METHOD

- Heat the oil in a non-stick *kadai* and add the mustard seeds and curry leaves. When the seeds begin to splutter, add the asafoetida, turmeric powder, onions and chillies. Stir on high heat for one minute.
- Add the pumpkin and salt. Cook, covered, on low heat for five to seven minutes, or till the pumpkin is tender.
- Add the lemon juice and mix well.

Rishipanchami Bhajee

Sodium Content
Per Serving: 306 mg

INGREDIENTS

1 medium ridge gourd, scraped and cut into 1-inch pieces

2 medium cucumbers, peeled and cut into 1-inch pieces

150 grams red pumpkin, peeled and cut into 1-inch pieces

½ small snake gourd, cut into 1-inch pieces

4-5 ladies' fingers, trimmed and cut into 4 pieces each

5-6 green chillies, stemmed and slit

2 tablespoons fresh grated coconut

½ level teaspoon salt

Seasoning

1 teaspoon cow's milk ghee

1 teaspoon cumin seeds

METHOD

- Place a deep non-stick pan on medium heat and add one and a half cups of water.
- Add the ridge gourd, cucumbers, red pumpkin, snake gourd, ladies' fingers, chillies and coconut and bring to a boil. Add salt and stir.
- Lower the heat, cover with a lid and simmer for eight to ten minutes or till vegetables are tender.
- Place a small non-stick pan over medium heat and add the ghee. Add the cumin seeds and when they start to change colour, pour the seasoning over the vegetables.
- Serve hot.

Spinach And Pumpkin Curry

Sodium Content Per Serving: 311 mg

INGREDIENTS

15-20 spinach leaves, shredded

200 grams red pumpkin, unpeeled and cut into small cubes

1 tablespoon pumpkin seeds with skin, roasted

2 teaspoons oil

½ teaspoon mustard seeds

10-12 curry leaves

2 medium onions, diced

1 inch ginger, cut into strips

3 green chillies, chopped

½ level teaspoon salt

½ teaspoon grated lemon rind

¼ teaspoon turmeric powder

½ teaspoon cumin powder

¼ cup soy milk

2 cups salt-free Vegetable Stock (page 103)

METHOD

- Heat the oil in a non-stick pan; add the mustard seeds and curry leaves. When the seeds splutter, add the onions and pumpkin, and sauté for two minutes.
- Add the ginger, green chillies and salt, and mix. Cover and cook for two minutes.
- Add the lemon rind, turmeric powder and cumin powder, and mix.
- Stir in the soy milk and vegetable stock, cover and cook till the pumpkin is soft and tender.
- Add the spinach and roasted pumpkin seeds and mix. Cook for four to five minutes longer.
- Serve hot.

Tawa Vegetables

Sodium Content Per Serving: 485 mg

INGREDIENTS

4 pointed gourds, halved

8 ivy gourds, halved

1 small bitter gourd, peeled, seeded and cut into strips

8 ladies' fingers, cut lengthways into four

8 shallots

6 button mushrooms, quartered

1 tablespoon oil

Gravy

1 tablespoon oil

3 medium onions, chopped

1 inch ginger, chopped

3 green chillies, seeded and chopped

½ teaspoon red chilli powder

1 teaspoon coriander powder

3 medium tomatoes, puréed

¾ level teaspoon salt

1 tablespoon lemon juice

2 tablespoons chopped fresh coriander

METHOD

- Steam the three types of gourds for four to five minutes. Set aside.
- Heat one tablespoon of oil in a non-stick *kadai*. Add the ladies' fingers and toss. Cook on medium heat for two minutes.
- Add the shallots and mushrooms, and cook for another two minutes. Mix together with the steamed gourds.
- For the gravy, heat the oil in another non-stick *kadai*. Add the chopped onions and ginger, and sauté for one minute.
- Stir in the green chillies, chilli powder, coriander powder, puréed tomatoes, salt and lemon juice. Cook for two minutes.
- Heat a non-stick *tawa*. Place half the cooked vegetables on the *tawa*, along with half the prepared gravy. Stir and cook until the vegetables are well coated.
- Repeat the process with the remaining vegetables and gravy. (You can sauté the vegetables in individual portions if you prefer.) Garnish with the chopped coriander.

Gobhi-Matar

Sodium Content Per Serving: 365 mg

INGREDIENTS

1 medium cauliflower, separated into florets

1 cup shelled green peas

1 tablespoon oil

1 teaspoon cumin seeds

1 teaspoon ginger paste

1 teaspoon garlic paste

2 teaspoons coriander powder

½ teaspoon red chilli powder

½ teaspoon turmeric powder

2 medium tomatoes, freshly puréed

½ level teaspoon salt

¾ teaspoon *garam masala* powder

½ teaspoon dried mango powder

1 green chilli, slit

METHOD

- Heat the oil in a non-stick *kadai* and add the cumin seeds. When they begin to change colour add the ginger paste and garlic paste. Sauté for half a minute.
- Add the coriander powder, chilli powder and turmeric powder. Sauté for another half a minute.
- Add the cauliflower florets, green peas, half a cup of water and tomato purée. Add the salt and mix. Cover and cook for eight to ten minutes, stirring occasionally
- Add the garam masala powder and dried mango powder and mix.
- Garnish with green chilli and serve hot.

Khumb-Hara Dhania

Sodium Content
Per Serving: 315 mg

INGREDIENTS

300 grams button mushrooms, cut into chunks

2 tablespoons chopped fresh coriander

1 tablespoon oil

3 green cardamoms

1 black cardamom

3 cloves

1 inch cinnamon

1 bay leaf

A pinch of ground mace

1 cup boiled onion paste (see below)

2 teaspoons ginger-garlic paste

2 green chillies, chopped

½ teaspoon red chilli powder

½ teaspoon coriander powder

½ cup skimmed milk yogurt, whisked

½ level teaspoon salt

1 inch ginger, cut into thin strips

METHOD

- Heat the oil in a non-stick *kadai*. Add the cardamoms, cloves, cinnamon, bay leaf and ground mace, and sauté over medium heat till fragrant.
- Add the onion paste and sauté for two to three minutes. Stir in the ginger-garlic paste and continue sautéing for half a minute. Add the chillies and sauté for half a minute longer
- Add the chilli powder and coriander powder, and sauté on low heat for a few seconds. Add the mushrooms and cook on low heat for seven to eight minutes.
- Remove from heat and stir in the yogurt and salt. Mix well and return the pan to the heat. Add one-fourth cup of water and bring to a boil. Lower heat and simmer for two minutes.
- Add the chopped coriander and simmer for five to six minutes.
- Transfer the mushrooms to a serving bowl and garnish with the ginger strips.

Chef's Tip: For the onion paste, peel and roughly chop 4–5 medium onions. Put them in a non-stick pan and add 1 bay leaf, 1 black cardamom and 50 ml water. Bring to a boil, and simmer till the onions are transparent and the liquid has evaporated. Cool; discard the bay leaf and cardamom. Transfer the onions to a blender and process to a fine purée.

Vazul Bandh Gubhi

Sodium Content Per Serving: 292 mg

INGREDIENTS

300 grams cabbage, chopped

1 tablespoon red chilli powder

¼ teaspoon asafoetida

1 tablespoon oil

1 teaspoon cumin seeds

¼ level teaspoon salt

¼ teaspoon turmeric powder

1 teaspoon dried ginger powder

1 tablespoon fennel powder

METHOD

- Mix the chilli powder with two tablespoons of water and set aside. Mix asafoetida in one teaspoon of water and set aside.
- Heat the oil in a non-stick pan; add the cumin seeds and when they change colour add the cabbage and sauté for two minutes.
- Add the salt, chilli powder-water mixture, asafoetida-water mixture and turmeric powder and mix well. Cover and cook till half done. Add a little water if required.
- Add the ginger powder and fennel powder, and cook till the cabbage is tender.
- Serve hot.

Khumb Shaslik

Sodium Content
Per Serving: 304 mg

INGREDIENTS

10-12 large fresh button mushrooms

1 medium onion, cut into 1½-inch pieces, layers separated

2 medium tomatoes, seeded and cut into 1½-inch pieces

2 medium green capsicums, cut into 1½-inch pieces

2 tablespoons drained (hung) skimmed yogurt

½ tablespoon Kashmiri red chilli powder

1 teaspoon *garam masala* powder

1 teaspoon crushed dried fenugreek leaves

2 teaspoons ginger paste

2 teaspoons garlic paste

½ level teaspoon salt

2 teaspoons cow's milk ghee

METHOD

- Mix together the drained yogurt, chilli powder, *garam masala* powder, dried fenugreek leaves, ginger paste, garlic paste and salt, and mix well. Cut the stems of the mushrooms and add to the yogurt mixture along with the onion, tomatoes and green capsicum. Marinate for half an hour.
- Thread them onto skewers in the following order – onion, mushroom, green capsicum and tomato. Repeat once ending with a piece of onion.
- Place the skewers on the barbecue and roast, basting with ghee from time to time. Rotate the skewers a few times so that the vegetables cook evenly on all sides.
- Serve hot.

Sai Bhaji

Sodium Content
Per Serving: 453 mg

INGREDIENTS

750 grams fresh spinach leaves, chopped

50 grams dill leaves, chopped

50 grams roselle leaves, chopped

50 grams fresh fenugreek leaves, chopped

½ cup split Bengal gram, soaked and drained

4 teaspoons oil

2 teaspoons cumin seeds

1 inch ginger, chopped

10 garlic cloves, chopped

3 green chillies, chopped

1 large onion, roughly chopped

3 medium tomatoes, roughly chopped

2 baby brinjals, cut into 8 pieces

1 small potato, cut into 1-inch cubes

1 teaspoon red chilli powder

1 teaspoon turmeric powder

2 tablespoons coriander powder

½ level teaspoon salt

METHOD

- Heat the oil in a deep non-stick pan. Add the cumin seeds and sauté for thirty seconds.
- Add the ginger and garlic and sauté for thirty seconds. Add the chillies and sauté for thirty seconds.
- Add the onion and sauté. Add the tomatoes and sauté. Add the drained split Bengal gram, brinjals and potato and stir.
- Add the chilli powder, turmeric powder, coriander powder and salt and sauté for five minutes.
- Add the spinach, dill, roselle and fenugreek leaves, one after the other and sauté for two minutes.
- Add two and a half cups of water and simmer for forty minutes or till the split Bengal gram is cooked.
- Blend with a hand blender for one to two minutes.
- Transfer the sai *bhaji* into a serving bowl and serve hot with steamed rice.

Tofu-Chana Dal

Sodium Content Per Serving: 319 mg

INGREDIENTS

¾ cup split Bengal gram

200 grams bean curd (tofu), cut into small cubes

1 teaspoon oil

½ teaspoon mustard seeds

10–12 curry leaves

2 pinches of asafoetida

½ level teaspoon salt

¼ teaspoon turmeric powder

1 tablespoon lemon juice

¼ cup roughly torn fresh mint

METHOD

- Soak the Bengal gram in two cups of water for three to four hours. Drain and set aside.
- Heat the oil in a non-stick pan and add the mustard seeds and curry leaves. When the seeds begin to splutter, stir in the asafoetida. Add the drained Bengal gram and salt, and sauté for two minutes.
- Stir in the turmeric powder and half a cup of water. Cover, and cook for ten to twelve minutes, or until the Bengal gram is soft.
- Add the tofu, lemon juice and fresh mint. Cook for half a minute, remove from heat and serve.

Aloo-Gobhi Adraki

Sodium Content Per Serving: 368 mg

INGREDIENTS

1 medium potato, cut into 1-inch cubes

1 medium cauliflower, separated into large florets

1 tablespoon oil

1 teaspoon cumin seeds

2 green chillies, slit

1 tablespoon ginger paste

¼ teaspoon turmeric powder

½ teaspoon red chilli powder

½ level teaspoon salt

2 tablespoons skimmed milk yogurt

2-inches ginger, cut into thin strips

1 small tomato, chopped

2 tablespoons chopped fresh coriander

METHOD

- Heat the oil in a non-stick pan and add the cumin seeds. When the seeds begin to change colour, add the green chillies and ginger paste. Sauté for half a minute. Add the potato and cauliflower, and sauté for two to three minutes.
- Add the turmeric powder, chilli powder and salt, and mix. Add the yogurt and mix again. Cover and cook on medium heat till the vegetables are tender.
- Add the ginger strips and chopped tomato, and stir to mix. Cook for a few minutes till the tomatoes are soft.
- Garnish with chopped coriander and serve hot.

Chef's Tip: You can add half a cup of green peas for a different flavour.

Chicken Haleem

Sodium Content Per Serving: 497 mg

INGREDIENTS

4 boneless chicken breasts (450 grams), cut into ½-inch cubes

2 tablespoons cow's milk ghee

2-3 green cardamoms

5-6 cloves

1 inch cinnamon

2 bay leaves

1 teaspoon cumin seeds

3 medium onions, sliced

1 tablespoon ginger paste

1 tablespoon garlic paste

2 tablespoons split green gram, soaked

2 tablespoons split Bengal gram, soaked

3 tablespoons broken wheat, soaked

½ teaspoon turmeric power

¾ teaspoon red chilli powder

¾ level teaspoon salt

½ teaspoon *garam masala* powder

2 tablespoons chopped fresh coriander

10-12 fresh mint leaves, roughly torn

1 tablespoon lemon juice

METHOD

- Heat the ghee in a deep non-stick pan. Add the green cardamoms, cloves, cinnamon, bay leaves, cumin seeds and onions, and sauté till light brown.
- Add the ginger paste and garlic paste, and continue to sauté.
- Add the green gram, Bengal gram and the broken wheat, and stir. Add the turmeric powder and chilli powder, and mix. Add half a cup of water and sauté for two to three minutes.
- Add the chicken and salt, and mix. Add four cups water and bring the mixture to a boil.
- Add the *garam masala* powder, chopped coriander, mint leaves and lemon juice. Stir and cover the pan. Cook on medium heat till the chicken is tender.
- Remove the bay leaves. Purée the chicken and gravy preferably with a hand blender and serve hot.

Fish Moilee

Sodium Content Per Serving: 418 mg

INGREDIENTS

600 grams pomfret, cut into ½-inch thick slices

½ level teaspoon salt

1 teaspoon turmeric powder

2 teaspoons lemon juice

1 tablespoon oil

1 teaspoon mustard seeds

8-10 curry leaves

2 medium onions, chopped

2 teaspoons ginger paste

2 teaspoons garlic paste

3 green chillies, slit

1 cup thin Coconut Milk (page 103)

METHOD

- Apply a little of the salt, turmeric powder and lemon juice on the fish slices, and set aside for fifteen minutes.
- Heat the oil in a non-stick *kadai*; add the mustard seeds. When they splutter, add the curry leaves and sauté for a few seconds. Add the onions and cook until soft and translucent.
- Add the ginger paste, garlic paste, green chillies and fish slices. Cook on high heat for half a minute.
- Add the coconut milk and the remaining salt. Cook, covered, on low heat for about ten minutes.
- Serve hot with steamed rice.

Green Chilli-Chicken

Sodium Content Per Serving: 710 mg

INGREDIENTS

600 grams chicken on the bone, cut into 1½-inch pieces

½ cup small green chillies

2 green chillies, roughly chopped

2 small onions, roughly chopped

10 garlic cloves

1½ inch ginger, sliced

½ cup chopped fresh coriander

1 tablespoon oil

½ teaspoon cumin seeds

¼ teaspoon turmeric powder

½ teaspoon cumin powder

2 teaspoons coriander powder

1 level teaspoon salt

½ teaspoon *garam masala* powder

METHOD

- Grind together two roughly chopped green chillies, onions, garlic, ginger and chopped coriander. Add the mixture to the chicken and marinate for about half an hour.
- Heat the oil in a non-stick wok or *kadai* and add the cumin seeds. When they begin to change colour, add the turmeric powder.
- Add the marinated chicken and half cup of small green chillies, and mix well. Add the cumin powder and coriander powder, and mix well.
- Add the salt and garam masala powder, and mix again. Add half a cup of water and mix. Cover and cook on medium heat for eight to ten minutes.
- Lower the heat and cook for another eight to ten minutes, or till the chicken is tender.
- Serve hot.

Kachchi Mirchi Ka Murgh

Sodium Content Per Serving: 310 mg

INGREDIENTS

800 grams chicken, cut into 2-inch pieces on the bone

10-12 small Bhavnagri chillies

2 teaspoons fennel powder

½ teaspoon fenugreek seed powder

2 teaspoons roasted cumin powder

2 teaspoons yellow mustard seeds, crushed

½ teaspoon onion seeds

½ level teaspoon salt

¾ cup skimmed milk yogurt, whisked

2 green chillies, crushed

2 teaspoons oil

2 medium onions, sliced

1 tablespoon ginger paste

1 tablespoon garlic paste

1 tablespoon coriander powder

½ teaspoon turmeric powder

½ teaspoon red chilli powder

METHOD

- Slit the chillies and remove seeds.
- In a bowl, mix together fennel powder, fenugreek seed powder, roasted cumin powder, crushed yellow mustard seeds, onion seeds and one-fourth teaspoon salt. Stuff the mixture into the slit chillies and set aside.
- Place the chicken in a bowl. Add the remaining salt, yogurt and crushed green chillies and leave to marinate for about fifteen minutes.
- Heat the oil in a non-stick pan. Add the onions and sauté till they soften. Add the stuffed chillies and mix.
- Add the ginger paste, garlic paste, coriander powder, turmeric powder, and chilli powder and sauté for two to three minutes. Cover and cook till the chillies soften.
- Add the marinated chicken and mix well. Cover and cook on high heat for about ten minutes.
- Uncover the pan and stir once. Cover and cook on low heat for another ten minutes.
- Serve hot.

Saagwala Gosht

Sodium Content Per Serving: 414 mg

INGREDIENTS

500 grams spinach

600 grams mutton on the bone, cut into 1½-inch pieces

5 green chillies

2 tablespoons oil

2 bay leaves

6 green cardamoms

2 black cardamoms

1 inch stick cinnamon

4 cloves

1 teaspoon cumin seeds

3 medium onions, sliced

6-8 garlic cloves, chopped

1 tablespoon ginger paste

1 tablespoon garlic paste

1 teaspoon red chilli powder

½ level teaspoon salt

1 inch piece ginger, cut into thin strips

METHOD

- Blanch the spinach in boiling water for one minute. Drain well. Grind it with the green chillies to a coarse paste.
- Heat the oil in a thick-bottomed non-stick pan. Add the bay leaves, green cardamoms, black cardamoms, cinnamon, cloves and cumin seeds. When cumin seeds begin to change colour, add the onions. Sauté till the onions are translucent. Add the chopped garlic and continue to sauté for another minute.
- Add the ginger paste, garlic paste, chilli powder and mutton. Cook on high heat, stirring continuously for three to four minutes. Add three cups of water and cook covered until mutton is almost done.
- Add the salt and spinach paste, and cook till mutton is fully blended with spinach and is tender.
- Serve hot, garnished with ginger strips.

Tamatar-Murgh Kofta

Sodium Content Per Serving: 357 mg

INGREDIENTS

4 boneless chicken breasts (450 grams), skinned

1 green chilli, chopped

1 tablespoon chopped fresh coriander

½ level teaspoon salt

5-6 medium tomatoes, quartered

1 medium onion, sliced

1½ tablespoons ginger paste

1 tablespoon garlic paste

1 teaspoon red chilli powder

2 teaspoons coriander powder

1 teaspoon roasted cumin powder

1 teaspoon oil

½ teaspoon mustard seeds

8-10 curry leaves

2 teaspoons rice flour

½ teaspoon *garam masala* powder

METHOD

- Roughly cut the chicken breasts into small pieces, and process in a blender along with the green chilli, chopped coriander and salt, until smooth and finely minced.
- Divide the minced chicken into ten to twelve equal portions, shape into balls and refrigerate until required.
- Pressure-cook the tomatoes for five to six minutes along with the onion, ginger and garlic pastes, chilli powder, coriander and cumin powders and one cup of water. Remove the lid when the pressure has reduced completely; cool the contents to room temperature, and process to a fine purée.
- Heat the oil in a non-stick pan and add the mustard seeds. When they splutter, add the curry leaves and stir-fry briefly. Stir in the tomato purée and one cup of water, and bring to a boil.
- Lower the heat and gently slide in the prepared chicken balls. Cover the pan with a tight-fitting lid and cook on low heat for fifteen minutes.
- Mix the rice flour in two to three tablespoons of water and add to the pan, stirring continuously. Simmer for five minutes.
- Sprinkle the *garam masala* powder and serve.

Patiala Gosht

Sodium Content
Per Serving: 363 mg

INGREDIENTS

750 grams boneless mutton, cut into 1½-inch cubes

3 inches ginger

10 garlic cloves, chopped

4 teaspoons cow's milk ghee

2 large onions, chopped

½ level teaspoon salt

4 black cardamoms

5 cloves

2 bay leaves

2 inches cinnamon

6 black peppercorns, crushed

1 teaspoon red chilli powder

½ teaspoon turmeric powder

1 tablespoon coriander powder

2 medium tomatoes, chopped

1½ teaspoons cumin seeds, pounded

METHOD

- Roughly chop the ginger and grind one-third of it with garlic.
- Heat the ghee in a deep non-stick pan; add the mutton, onions, ginger-garlic paste and salt, and sauté over low heat for about ten minutes.
- Add the black cardamoms, cloves, bay leaves, cinnamon and crushed peppercorns, and sauté for half a minute.
- Add two cups of water, cover and simmer, stirring occasionally, until mutton is tender.
- Remove the mutton from the gravy with a slotted spoon and set aside.
- Add the chilli powder, turmeric powder and coriander powder to the gravy and stir.
- Increase the heat, add the tomatoes and cook till soft and pulpy. Add one cup of water and simmer.
- Thread a piece of ginger between two mutton pieces onto two-inch tooth picks and place in the gravy. Simmer for five minutes, turning the tooth picks at regular intervals.
- Add the cumin powder and stir for a minute.
- Arrange the tooth picks on a flat dish, pour the gravy over and serve hot.

Akhrot Murgh

Sodium Content Per Serving: 516 mg

INGREDIENTS

¼ cup walnuts, blanched, peeled and powdered

400 grams boneless chicken, cut into ½-inch pieces

1 tablespoon ginger paste

1 tablespoon garlic paste

¾ level teaspoon salt

1 teaspoon cumin powder

4 tablespoons lemon juice

1 tablespoon oil

1 medium onion, grated

1 large tomato, puréed

4 green chillies, chopped

1 teaspoon coriander powder

2 tablespoons skimmed milk

2 pinches *garam masala* powder

METHOD

- Place the chicken in a bowl. Add the ginger paste, garlic paste, salt, half a teaspoon of cumin powder and lemon juice, and mix well. Marinate the chicken for half an hour.
- Heat the oil in a non-stick pan; add the onion and sauté till light brown. Add the tomato purée, mix well and continue to sauté for two to three minutes.
- Add the green chillies and cook for two minutes. Add the coriander powder, remaining cumin powder, mix well and cook for one more minute.
- Add the marinated chicken, mix well, cover and cook till tender.
- Add the walnuts, cook for two to three minutes on low heat. Add the milk and *garam masala* powder, and mix well. Simmer for two more minutes.
- Serve hot.

Bhapa Ilish

Sodium Content Per Serving: 421 mg

INGREDIENTS

1 kilogram hilsa (ilish)

1 teaspoon turmeric powder

1 teaspoon yellow mustard seeds

1 teaspoon black mustard seeds

2-3 green chillies, chopped

1 inch ginger, chopped

½ level teaspoon salt

1 tablespoon mustard oil

METHOD

- Wash the fish well and clean and gut it. Cut into slices across the bone (darnes). Sprinkle with the turmeric powder.
- Make a smooth paste of yellow mustard seeds, black mustard seeds, green chillies, ginger and salt. Apply the paste liberally on fish.
- In a pressure cooker, add three cups of water and place a ring in it. Take a non-stick platter and place the fish in it. Pour the mustard oil on top. Place the platter on the ring in the pressure cooker.
- Cover with the lid and steam for eight to ten minutes without the weight.
- Serve hot.

Masala Pomfret

Sodium Content Per Serving: 828 mg

INGREDIENTS

2 (600 grams each) fresh pomfrets

1 level teaspoon salt

Crushed black peppercorns to taste

1 teaspoon red chilli powder

½ teaspoon turmeric powder

4 teaspoons oil

1 tablespoon garlic paste

1 tablespoon red chilli paste

1 tablespoon fresh coriander paste

1 tablespoon Tamarind Pulp (page 103)

½ teaspoon clove powder

A pinch of asafoetida

½ cup semolina

1 tablespoon chopped fresh coriander

METHOD

- Make half-inch deep slits on either side of the pomfrets. Rub the pomfrets with a mixture of half level teaspoon salt, crushed peppercorns, chilli powder and turmeric powder.
- Mix together two teaspoons oil, the garlic paste, chilli paste, fresh coriander paste, tamarind pulp, clove powder, asafoetida and remaining salt. Rub the mixture on the pomfrets. Set aside for fifteen minutes.
- Heat a non-stick *tawa*. Roll each pomfret in the semolina and place on the *tawa*. Drizzle half a teaspoon of oil all round the fish and cook for two to three minutes.
- When the underside is golden, flip over, drizzle another half teaspoon of oil all round and cook till the other side is evenly golden.
- Garnish with chopped coriander and serve hot.

Quick Jeera Chicken

Sodium Content Per Serving: 397 mg

INGREDIENTS

½ teaspoon cumin seeds

800 grams chicken, cut into 1½ -inch pieces

1 tablespoon lemon juice

2 tablespoons oil

4 green chillies, broken into two

½ cup skimmed milk yogurt

1 tablespoon chopped fresh coriander

½ level teaspoon salt

½ cup fresh mint leaves, hand torn

METHOD

- Apply lemon juice to the chicken and mix well.
- Heat the oil in a non-stick pan; add the cumin seeds. When they begin to change colour, add the green chillies and sauté for a minute.
- Add the chicken and roast for a while. Add the yogurt and chopped coriander. Cover and cook till the chicken is nearly done. Add salt; stir and continue to cook.
- Add mint leaves, stir and serve hot.

Bhindi-Gosht

Sodium Content Per Serving: 477 mg

INGREDIENTS

250 grams ladies' fingers, trimmed

400 grams mutton on the bone, cut into small pieces

1 tablespoon cow's milk ghee

1 teaspoon cumin seeds

2 one-inch cinnamon sticks

4 black cardamoms

8-10 black peppercorns

2 medium onions, thinly sliced

3 green chillies, slit

1 teaspoon ginger paste

1 teaspoon garlic paste

¾ level teaspoon salt

½ teaspoon turmeric powder

2 teaspoons coriander powder

1 tablespoon oil

2 medium tomatoes, puréed

½ teaspoon red chilli powder

½ teaspoon *garam masala* powder

4 tablespoons chopped fresh coriander

METHOD

- Heat the ghee in a pressure cooker. Add half a teaspoon of cumin seeds, cinnamon, black cardamoms, peppercorns and onions, and sauté till lightly browned.
- Add the mutton and green chillies, and continue to sauté. Add the ginger paste, garlic paste, salt, turmeric powder and coriander powder, and stir.
- Heat the oil in a non-stick *kadai*. Add the remaining cumin seeds. Make a slit lengthways on one side of the ladies' fingers and add to the *kadai*. Sauté till light brown and set aside.
- Add two cups of water to the mutton and mix. Add the tomato purée and stir.
- Add the chilli powder and *garam masala* powder, and mix well.
- Add the chopped coriander and the sautéed ladies' fingers, and mix well.
- Seal the cooker with the lid and cook till the pressure is released once (one whistle). Reduce heat to medium and cook for twenty to twenty-five minutes.
- Open the cooker when the pressure reduces completely. Serve hot.

Char Dal Ni Khichdi

Sodium Content
Per Serving: 293 mg

INGREDIENTS

1½ tablespoons split pigeon peas, soaked

1½ tablespoons split field beans, soaked

1½ tablespoons skinless split green gram, soaked

1½ tablespoons split red lentils, soaked for an hour

¾ cup rice, soaked

1 tablespoon cow's milk ghee

6- 8 cloves

2-inch stick cinnamon

3-4 black cardamoms

2 medium onions, sliced

A pinch of asafoetida

1 teaspoon chopped ginger

1 teaspoon turmeric powder

½ level teaspoon salt

METHOD

- Heat the ghee in a non-stick pan; add cloves, cinnamon, black cardamoms and onions, and sauté till onions turn brown.
- Add the asafoetida, ginger and turmeric powder, and mix well. Add the rice and all the pulses and sauté for three to four minutes.
- Add the salt and five cups of water. When the mixture comes to a boil, lower the heat, cover and cook till done. If the khichdi looks too dry, sprinkle a little water, cover and cook for five more minutes.
- Serve hot.

Baoli Handi

Sodium Content
Per Serving: 456 mg

INGREDIENTS

1 cup rice (kolam), soaked

1 medium onion, sliced

1 medium carrot, cut into ½-inch pieces

3-4 small cauliflower florets

¼ cup shelled green peas

3 green chillies, chopped

3-4 French beans, cut into ½-inch pieces

1 tablespoon oil

1 teaspoon cumin seeds

¾ level teaspoon salt

½ teaspoon turmeric powder

¾ teaspoon red chilli powder

¼ cup soya granules, soaked and drained

1 small tomato, chopped

1 tablespoon fresh coriander, chopped

¼ cup skinless split green gram, soaked and drained

4-5 spinach leaves, roughly torn

METHOD

- Heat the oil in a deep non-stick pan. Add the cumin seeds and when they begin to change colour, add the onion, carrot, cauliflower, green peas, green chillies and French beans. Sauté for two minutes.
- Add the salt, turmeric powder and chilli powder, and mix well. Cover and cook on low heat for three to four minutes.
- Add the rice and three cups of water. Cover and cook for two minutes.
- Add the soya granules, stir and cook, covered, for two minutes.
- Add the tomato, chopped coriander, green gram and spinach leaves, and stir to mix well. Cover and cook on medium heat till the vegetables are tender.
- Serve hot.

Vegetable Pulao

Sodium Content Per Serving: 442 mg

INGREDIENTS

1 medium carrot, cut into ¼-inch cubes

½ cup shelled green peas

1½ cups rice, soaked

2 tablespoons oil

2-3 bay leaves

1 teaspoon cumin seeds

¾ level teaspoon salt

METHOD

- Heat the oil in a non-stick pan. Add the bay leaves and cumin seeds, and sauté till light brown.
- Add the carrot and peas, and sauté for a few minutes. If using frozen peas, add them after the carrots are slightly cooked.
- Drain the rice and add to the above mixture, and sauté for half a minute. Add two cups of water and salt, and mix well.
- When the water comes to a boil, lower the heat and cook, covered, till the rice is tender.
- Serve hot.

Beetroot-Kakdi Magaj Pulao

Sodium Content Per Serving: 311 mg

INGREDIENTS

1½ cups rice, soaked

1 medium beetroot, grated

2 teaspoons cucumber seeds (kakdi magaz)

1 tablespoon pure ghee

2 bay leaves

3-4 cloves

2 medium onions, sliced

1 teaspoon red chilli powder

½ level teaspoon salt

A few sprigs fresh mint leaves, for garnishing

METHOD

- Heat the ghee in a thick-bottomed non-stick pan; add the bay leaves and cloves, and sauté for a few seconds. Add the onions and sauté for two minutes.
- Add the cucumber seeds and continue to sauté for one minute.
- Add the beetroot and sauté for two more minutes. Add the chilli powder and sauté for around two minutes.
- Add the drained rice and sauté for three to four minutes.
- Add three cups of water and salt, and mix well. When the mixture comes to a boil, cover and reduce heat. Cook till the rice is tender.
- Garnish with mint sprigs and serve hot.

Cauliflower And Lemon Rice

Sodium Content Per Serving: 472 mg

INGREDIENTS

300 grams cauliflower, separated into florets

2 tablespoons lemon juice

2 cups brown Basmati rice

¾ level teaspoon salt

4 green chillies, roughly chopped

3 dried red chillies, broken into half

2 tablespoons coriander seeds

¼ teaspoon turmeric powder

1 teaspoon oil

¼ teaspoon mustard seeds

½ teaspoon skinless split black gram

⅛ teaspoon fenugreek seeds

A pinch of asafoetida

7–8 curry leaves

METHOD

- Soak the rice in four cups of water for two hours. Drain and cook in six cups of water until just cooked, ensuring that each grain is separate. Drain and set aside.
- Mix the salt with the lemon juice.
- Grind the green and red chillies, coriander seeds and turmeric powder to a fine paste, adding water as required.
- Heat the oil in a non-stick *kadai*. Add the mustard seeds, split black gram and fenugreek seeds, and sauté till the gram turns light brown. Stir in the asafoetida and curry leaves, and sauté for thirty seconds.
- Add the *masala* paste and cauliflower, and mix well. Sprinkle water, cover the *kadai* and cook on low heat till cauliflower is soft. Add the rice and lemon juice mixture, and mix lightly. Cover and cook until everything is heated through.

Kolambi Bhaat

Sodium Content Per Serving: 334 mg

INGREDIENTS

1½ cups brown rice

10 medium prawns, shelled and deveined

1 teaspoon lemon juice

½ level teaspoon salt

1 tablespoon chopped fresh coriander

1 tablespoon grated fresh coconut

3 green chillies, chopped

½ inch piece ginger, finely chopped

4 garlic cloves, finely chopped

12–15 fresh mint leaves

¾ tablespoon oil

1-inch stick cinnamon

3 black cardamoms

1 star anise

3 cloves

1 teaspoon cumin seeds

1 large onion, chopped

1½ tablespoons low-fat coconut milk

METHOD

- Soak the brown rice in two and a half cups of water for two hours. Drain and set aside.
- Marinate the prawns in the lemon juice and one-fourth teaspoon salt.
- Grind the chopped coriander with the coconut, green chillies, ginger, garlic and fresh mint to a fine paste.
- Heat the oil in a thick-bottomed non-stick pan; add the cinnamon, cardamoms, star anise, cloves and cumin seeds and sauté for one minute.
- Add the chopped onion and sauté until it turns a light golden brown. Add the *masala* paste and stir-fry for a few seconds.
- Add the rice and stir gently for one minute. Stir in the coconut milk and one litre of water. Bring to the boil, stirring once or twice and add the remaining salt. Cook on a medium heat until the water is absorbed.
- Add the prawns, reduce the heat and cook, covered, until the rice is tender.
- Remove the pan from the heat and serve hot.

Brown Rice Biryani With Chutney Chicken

Sodium Content Per Serving: 552 mg

INGREDIENTS

2 cups brown rice, soaked

½ cup fresh coriander paste

400 grams chicken on the bone, cut into1½-inch pieces

¾ level teaspoon salt

1 inch cinnamon

4 green cardamoms

6 cloves

5-6 saffron threads

2 tablespoons skimmed milk

½ cup skimmed milk yogurt

1 teaspoon lemon juice

¼ teaspoon turmeric powder

2 tablespoons cow's milk ghee

3 medium onions, sliced

1 teaspoon ginger paste

1 teaspoon garlic paste

3 tablespoons chopped fresh coriander

A few rose petals

A few sprigs of fresh mint

¾ teaspoon screw pine water

¾ teaspoon rose water

½ teaspoon *garam masala* powder

Wholewheat flour dough, as required

METHOD

- Cook the rice with half the salt, six cups of water, half the cinnamon, cardamoms and cloves till three-fourth done. Drain and set aside. Soak the saffron in the skimmed milk and set aside.
- In a bowl, mix together the fresh coriander paste, yogurt, remaining salt, lemon juice and turmeric powder. Marinate the chicken in it for an hour, preferably in a refrigerator.
- Heat one tablespoon ghee in a deep non-stick pan and sauté half the onions on medium heat till well browned. Drain and set aside.
- Add the remaining ghee to the same pan; add the remaining cinnamon, green cardamoms, cloves and the remaining onions, and sauté till the onions are light brown.
- Add the ginger paste and garlic paste, and sauté, adding a little water to avoid scorching. Add the marinated chicken, mix and cook. Reduce heat, cover and cook for five minutes. Add the chopped coriander.
- Spread a layer of half the brown rice at the base of a thick-bottomed non-stick pan. Sprinkle half the saffron-flavoured milk, rose petals, mint leaves, half the sautéed onions, screw pine water, rose water and *garam masala* powder. Spread the chicken gravy over the rice. Top with layers of the remaining brown rice, saffron-flavoured milk, rose petals, mint leaves, sautéed onions, screw pine water, rose water and *garam masala* powder. Cover the pan with a lid and seal with the dough.
- Heat a *tawa* and place the pan on it. Cook on medium heat for about half an hour. Serve hot with raita.

Chicken Pulao

Sodium Content Per Serving: 304 mg

INGREDIENTS

600 grams boneless chicken, cut into 1½-inch pieces

1½ cups Basmati rice, soaked

1 teaspoon red chilli powder

½ level teaspoon salt

1 tablespoon ginger paste

1 tablespoon garlic paste

1 tablespoon oil

1 teaspoon cumin seeds

6-8 cloves

6-8 green cardamoms

2 bay leaves

2 inches cinnamon

2 medium onions, sliced

3 medium tomatoes, chopped

2 tablespoons skimmed milk yogurt

3 cups unsalted chicken stock

METHOD

- Place the chicken in a bowl. Add half the chilli powder, one-fourth teaspoon salt, half the ginger paste, half the garlic paste, and mix well. Cover and place in the refrigerator for fifteen to twenty minutes to marinate.
- Heat the oil in a non-stick pan; add the cumin seeds, cloves, cardamoms, bay leaves and cinnamon and sauté till fragrant. Add the onions and sauté till lightly browned.
- Add the remaining ginger paste, garlic paste and chilli powder. Stir and sauté for two minutes.
- Add the tomatoes, remaining salt, yogurt and continue to sauté for two minutes.
- Add the rice, marinated chicken and mix well.
- Add chicken stock and bring to a boil. Cover, reduce heat and leave to cook till both the chicken and rice are tender.
- Serve hot.

Dal Bahar

Sodium Content Per Serving: 317 mg

INGREDIENTS

¾ cup split pigeon peas

1 medium carrot, cut into ½-inch pieces

3-4 French beans, cut into ½-inch pieces

1 drumstick, cut into 2-inch pieces

¼ small cauliflower, separated into small florets

1 teaspoon oil

½ teaspoon mustard seeds

1 teaspoon cumin seeds

6-8 curry leaves

A pinch of asafoetida (optional)

1-2 green chillies, slit

5-6 garlic cloves, chopped

1 inch piece ginger, chopped

½ teaspoon turmeric powder

½ teaspoon red chilli powder

½ level teaspoon salt

2 tablespoons chopped fresh coriander

1 tablespoon lemon juice

METHOD

- Soak the pigeon peas in two cups of water for an hour.
- Heat the oil in a pressure cooker. Add the mustard seeds, cumin seeds, curry leaves, asafoetida, slit green chillies, garlic and ginger, and sauté for a minute.
- Add the carrot, French beans, drumstick and soaked pigeon peas, and mix. Add the turmeric powder, chilli powder, salt and two cups of water, and bring to a boil.
- Add the cauliflower, stir and seal the cooker with the lid. Cook under pressure till the pressure is released once (one whistle).
- Remove the lid once the pressure has reduced completely. Mix lightly with the back of a ladle. Add the chopped coriander and lemon juice, and stir to mix.
- Serve hot.

Hari Mirchonwali Toovar Dal

Sodium Content Per Serving: 299 mg

INGREDIENTS

1 cup split pigeon peas

4 green chillies, cut into 1-inch pieces

½ teaspoon turmeric powder

1 teaspoon oil

½ teaspoon mustard seeds

1 teaspoon cumin seeds

A pinch of asafoetida

6-8 curry leaves

1 medium onion, chopped

1 inch ginger, chopped

½ level teaspoon salt

3 tablespoons chopped fresh coriander

METHOD

- Wash the pigeon peas in several changes of water; soak in three cups of water for thirty minutes.
- Drain and pressure-cook with three cups of water and turmeric powder till the pressure is released three times (three whistles). Lower the heat and simmer for five minutes.
- Heat the oil in a small non-stick pan; add the mustard seeds and cumin seeds. When the mustard seeds begin to splutter and cumin seeds begin to change colour, add the asafoetida, curry leaves and green chillies. Sauté for half a minute and add the onion and ginger. Sauté for three to four minutes.
- Mix in the boiled *dal* and salt. Add water to adjust the consistency and bring the *dal* to a boil. Lower the heat and simmer for five minutes.
- Serve hot, garnished with chopped coriander.

Kairi Ki Dal

Sodium Content
Per Serving: 306 mg

INGREDIENTS

3 tablespoons chopped unripe mango

¾ cup split pigeon peas, soaked

2 teaspoons oil

8 shallots

½ teaspoon mustard seeds

½ teaspoon cumin seeds

5 garlic cloves, sliced

4 dried red chillies, broken and seeded

15 curry leaves

½ level teaspoon salt

METHOD

- In a pan, bring the pigeon peas and three cups of water to a boil.
- Heat one teaspoon oil in a non-stick pan. Add the shallots and sauté till golden. Add the shallots to the boiling *dal* and continue to cook.
- Heat the remaining oil in another non-stick pan. Add the mustard seeds, cumin seeds and garlic, and sauté for a few seconds.
- Add the chillies and curry leaves and sauté for a few seconds longer. Add the mango cubes and continue to sauté. Sprinkle salt and cook till the mango pieces soften.
- Add the mango to the *dal* and mix well. Cover and cook for about ten minutes on medium heat.
- Serve hot.

Andhra Dal

Sodium Content Per Serving: 313 mg

INGREDIENTS

1 cup split pigeon peas, soaked

2 unripe bananas, cut into 1-inch cubes

2 teaspoons split Bengal gram, roasted

2 teaspoons coriander seeds, roasted

6-8 black peppercorns

2 teaspoons grated coconut

4 dried red chillies

2 tablespoons tamarind pulp

½ teaspoon turmeric powder

½ level teaspoon salt

2 teaspoons oil

½ teaspoon mustard seeds

½ teaspoon cumin seeds

6-8 curry leaves

A pinch of asafoetida

METHOD

- Pressure-cook the pigeon peas with the banana and two cups of water till the pressure is released three times (three whistles).
- Grind together the Bengal gram, coriander seeds, peppercorns, coconut, and chillies with the tamarind pulp to a smooth paste.
- In a deep non-stick pan, mix together the boiled *dal*, ground paste, turmeric powder and salt.
- Heat the oil in a small non-stick pan and add the mustard seeds. As they begin to splutter add the cumin seeds, curry leaves and asafoetida.
- Pour the seasoning over the *dal*. Bring the *dal* to a boil on high heat, stirring continuously. Adjust the consistency and cook for two minutes.
- Serve hot with rice.

Tur Dal Amti

**Sodium Content
Per Serving: 306 mg**

INGREDIENTS

1 cup split pigeon peas, soaked

1 tablespoon rice bran oil

¼ teaspoon cumin seeds

1 small onion, chopped

2 green chillies

A pinch of asafoetida

½ level teaspoon salt

1 teaspoon grated jaggery

2 teaspoons Tamarind Pulp (page 103)

½ teaspoon red chilli powder

½ teaspoon *goda masala*

1 teaspoon chopped fresh coriander

1 tablespoon grated coconut

METHOD

- Pressure-cook the pigeon peas with two cups of water till the pressure is released three to four times (three to four whistles). Remove the lid when the pressure has reduced completely. Mash the *dal* with back of a round ladle.
- Heat the oil in a deep non-stick pan. Add the cumin seeds and sauté till they begin to change colour. Add the onion, green chillies and asafoetida, and sauté till lightly browned.
- Add the cooked *dal* and two cups of water. Mix well and bring to a boil.
- Lower the heat, add the salt, jaggery, tamarind pulp, chilli powder and *goda masala* and simmer for four to five minutes.
- Garnish with chopped coriander and grated coconut, and serve hot.

Bhindi Ki Kadhi

Sodium Content Per Serving: 340 mg

INGREDIENTS

8-10 medium ladies' fingers, trimmed and halved

3 cups buttermilk (made from skimmed milk yogurt)

2 tablespoons gram flour

½ teaspoon green chilli paste

½ teaspoon ginger-garlic paste

1 tablespoon cow's milk ghee

1 tablespoon grated jaggery

½ level teaspoon salt

A pinch of asafoetida

½ teaspoon cumin seeds

2 cloves

1 inch cinnamon

7-8 curry leaves

METHOD

- Pour the buttermilk into a deep bowl. Add the gram flour and mix well with a whisk. Add the green chilli paste, ginger-garlic paste and one cup of water and whisk well.
- Heat half the ghee in a non-stick pan; add the ladies' fingers and sauté till they are almost tender. Meanwhile, transfer the buttermilk mixture into a pan and bring to a boil.
- Cook, on low heat, stirring continuously for five minutes. Add the jaggery and stir well. Add the sautéed ladies' fingers and continue to boil for another five to eight minutes. Add salt and stir well.
- Heat the remaining ghee in a non-stick pan. Add the asafoetida, cumin seeds, cloves, cinnamon and curry leaves. Sauté till the cumin seeds start changing colour. Pour over the kadhi, stir and serve hot.

Pudina Paranthe

Sodium Content Per Serving: 306 mg

INGREDIENTS

2 cups wholewheat flour

1 cup fresh mint leaves

½ level teaspoon salt

2 teaspoons oil

METHOD

- Wash and pat the mint leaves dry. Lightly roast half the leaves on a hot non-stick *tawa*. Cool, crush to a powder and set aside. Chop the remaining mint leaves finely.
- Place the wholewheat flour and salt in a bowl. Add the chopped mint leaves and a little water and knead into a stiff dough. Cover and rest the dough for twenty to twenty-five minutes.
- Divide the dough into six equal portions and shape into balls.
- Roll out each ball into a medium-sized *chapati* and brush with a little oil and sprinkle with some flour. Fold the *chapati* like a fan and twist it back into the form of a ball. Set aside for five minutes.
- Roll out each portion into a five to seven-inch round *parantha*. Cook on a hot non-stick *tawa* till both sides are lightly golden brown.
- Sprinkle crushed mint leaves on the hot *parantha* and serve.

Onion And Coriander Paranthe

Sodium Content Per Serving: 308 mg

INGREDIENTS

1¼ cups wholewheat flour

½ level teaspoon salt

2 tablespoons skimmed milk yogurt

2 medium onions, finely chopped

1 tablespoon chopped fresh coriander

2 green chillies, chopped

½ teaspoon red chilli powder

1 teaspoon cumin powder

Cow's milk ghee for frying

METHOD

- Sift the flour with salt. Make a soft dough with flour, yogurt and half a cup of water. Cover with a damp cloth and set aside for half an hour.
- For the stuffing, mix together chopped onion, coriander, green chillies, chilli powder and cumin powder in a bowl.
- Knead the dough again and divide into four equal portions. Shape into balls and flatten between your palms.
- Roll out each ball into three-inch rounds, making the edges thinner than the centre.
- Place a portion of the stuffing in the centre, gather the edges together and shape once again into a ball.
- Roll each ball out into a seven-inch round *parantha*.
- Heat a non-stick *tawa* and place a *parantha* on it. Turn over once and drizzle a little ghee over it. Turn over again and spread a little ghee on the other side. Cook till both sides are cooked and golden.
- Serve hot.

Dalia Aur Dal Paranthe

Sodium Content Per Serving: 310 mg

INGREDIENTS

¾ cup broken wheat

¼ cup whole green gram, soaked

1 cup wholewheat flour

½ level teaspoon salt

1 inch ginger, grated

½ cup fresh coriander, finely chopped

1-2 green chillies, finely chopped

2 teaspoons cow's milk ghee

METHOD

- Pressure-cook the broken wheat and whole green gram in one and a half cups of water until soft. Cool and mash the mixture.
- Mix together the flour and salt. Add the cooked broken wheat-green gram mixture, ginger, chopped coriander and green chillies. Add water, if required, a little at a time and knead into a soft, pliable dough. Cover the dough with a damp cloth and set aside for fifteen minutes.
- Divide the dough into eight equal portions and shape into balls. Roll out each portion into a thin five to six-inch *parantha*.
- Brush a little ghee on a hot non-stick *tawa* and place a *parantha* on it and cook on medium heat for half a minute on each side. Lower the heat and cook till both sides are slightly brown.
- Serve hot.

Rajgire Ka Thepla

Sodium Content Per Serving: 332 mg

INGREDIENTS

1 cup amaranth seed flour

1 cup wholewheat flour

½ level teaspoon salt

1 inch ginger, grated

½ teaspoon sesame seeds

2 green chillies, finely chopped

2 tablespoons chopped fresh coriander

2 tablespoons skimmed milk yogurt

2 tablespoons cow's milk ghee

METHOD

- Place both the flours in a bowl. Mix in the salt, ginger, sesame seeds, green chillies and chopped coriander.
- Knead into a semi-soft dough with the yogurt and a little water. Cover with a damp cloth and set aside for half an hour.
- Divide into ten to twelve equal portions and shape into balls. Dust with flour and pat each ball into a *thepla*. If you can, roll it out with a rolling pin.
- Heat a *tawa*. Cook the *thepla* on both sides in a little ghee till light brown and crisp. Serve hot.

Jawari Bhakri

Sodium Content Per Serving: 20 mg

INGREDIENTS

2 cups sorghum flour

A pinch of salt

METHOD

- Mix the sorghum flour and salt. Add enough water to make soft dough. Knead well.
- Divide into eight equal portions and shape into round balls.
- Heat a *tawa* till moderately hot.
- Roll out each portion of the dough into a thin round. Cook on the *tawa* until the underside is cooked.
- Brush with a little water and flip over. Cook till golden brown.
- Remove and serve hot.

Masala Missi Roti

Sodium Content Per Serving: 167 mg

INGREDIENTS

1 cup gram flour

1 cup wholewheat flour

4 green chillies, chopped

1 medium onion, chopped

1 teaspoon turmeric powder

¼ level teaspoon salt

1 teaspoon dried mango powder

1 tablespoon ghee + for greasing

METHOD

- Sift together the two flours. Add the rest of the ingredients, plus enough water to form a soft dough. Knead till the dough is smooth. Rest the dough for ten minutes, covered with a damp cloth.
- Divide the dough into sixteen equal portions and shape into balls.
- Grease the palms of your hands and also the worktop. Place a dough ball on the worktop and press it down a little to form a round.
- Slightly moisten one palm of the hand and, using both hands, pat the dough between them to make a *roti*. Alternatively, roll out each ball of dough on a lightly floured surface, to make a six-inch *roti*
- Roast the *roti* on a hot non-stick *tawa*. Cook till light brown on both sides and serve hot.

Coconut Milk

Process 1 cup grated fresh coconut in a blender with ¼ cup warm water. Pass the ground coconut through a piece of muslin or strainer pressing firmly to extract all the juice, or first milk. Add a ¼ cup of warm water to the strained coconut to get the second, thinner milk from the same solids.

Date and Tamarind Chutney

Wash, stone and chop 15-20 dates. Dry-roast 2 teaspoons cumin seeds and ¼ teaspoon fennel seeds. Cool and grind to a powder. Cook the dates, 1 cup tamarind pulp, cumin and fennel powder, ½ cup jaggery, 2 teaspoons red chilli powder, 1 teaspoon dried ginger powder, black salt, salt and four cups of water till thick.

Tamarind Pulp

Soak 75 grams tamarind in 100 ml warm water for 10-15 minutes. Grind to a smooth paste and strain to remove any fibres. Store in an airtight container in the refrigerator.

Vegetable Stock

Peel, wash and chop 1 onion, ½ medium carrot, 2-3 inch celery stalk and 2-3 garlic cloves. Place in a pan with 1 bay leaf, 5-6 peppercorns, 2-3 cloves and 5 cups of water and bring to a boil. Lower heat and simmer for 15 minutes and strain. Cool and store in a refrigerator till further use.

Glossary

English	Hindi
Red lentils, split	Masoor dal
Amaranth seeds	Rajgira
Asafoetida	Hing
Bay leaves	Tej patta
Beaten rice	Poha
Bengal gram, split	Chana dal
Bottle gourd	Lauki
Broken wheat	Dalia
Brown gram	Moth
Buttermilk	Chhaach
Capsicum	Shimla mirch
Cardamom, black	Badi elaichi
Carom seeds	Ajwain
Carrots	Gajar
Chillies, red dried	Sookhi lal mirch
Cinnamon	Dalchini
Cloves	Laung
Coconut, fresh	Nariyal
Colocasia leaves	Arbi ke patte
Coriander seeds	Dhania
Cucumber	Kakdi
Cucumber seeds	Kakdi magaz
Cumin seeds	Jeera
Curry leaves	Kadhi patta
Dill	Suva bhaji
Dried mango powder	Amchur
Fennel	Saunf
Fenugreek leaves	Methi
Fenugreek seeds	Methi dana
Field beans, split	Waal ki dal
Gram flour	Besan
Green gram	Sabut moong
Green gram, split	Chhilkewali moong dal
Green gram, skinless, split	Dhuli moong dal
Green peas	Matar
Honey	Shahad
Ivy gourd	Kundru
Jaggery	Gur
Onion seeds	Kalonji
Ladies' Finger	Bhindi
Lettuce	Salad ke patte
Mint	Pudina
Mushroom	Khumb
Mustard seeds	Rai
Orange	Santara
Peppercorns, black	Kali mirch
Pigeon peas, split	Arhar dal/ toovar dal
Pointed gourd	Parwal
Puffed rice	Murmura
Raisins	Kishmish
Ridge gourd	Turai
Rose water	Gulab jal
Roselle leaves	Khatta bhaji
Saffron	Kesar
Screw opine water	Kewra jal
Semolina	Sooji/rawa
Sesame seed	Til
Shallots	Chhhote pyaaz
Spinach	Palak
Star anise	Chakri phool
Sweet lime	Mosambi
Tamarind	Imli
Unripe green mango	Keri
Walnuts	Akhrot
Watermelon	Tarbooj
Wholewheat flour	Atta
Yogurt	Dahi